The surgeon BURNOUT CURE

Mental Wellness for busy Lives

A guide written for the Surgeon's life

For every surgeon who has given everything to the OR and quietly wondered if there is anything left for themselves

Robert Amajoyi, MD
Ebere Jill Azumah, MD MPH

To my soulmate —

who held everything together
while I held the scalpel.

For my children —

who understood the absences
better than they should have had to.

For my youngest — Luke

who thinks surgeons are superheroes.
Son, the cape was always yours.

Thank you
Rob and Ebere

FOREWORD

There is a particular kind of grief that physicians rarely speak aloud — the grief of losing yourself inside the very vocation you sacrificed everything to enter. It does not arrive with ceremony. It accumulates. First as exhaustion that sleep no longer resolves. Then as a creeping indifference toward patients you once ached to serve. Then, in its most devastating form, as the quiet conviction that what you are doing no longer matters — or that you no longer matter within it. We call this burnout. But the word is almost too clean, too clinical, for what it actually is: the systemic erosion of the human being underneath the physician.

I have spent years watching this erosion — in residents I have trained, in colleagues I have admired, and at times, in the mirror. The data is not abstract to those of us in academic medicine and surgical training. We know that burnout affects nearly half of practicing physicians. We know that a meta-analysis of more than 42,000 physicians demonstrated a doubled risk of complications in the care delivered by burned-out clinicians. We know that 14 percent of physicians have reported suicidal ideation — a figure that should stop every medical leader cold. These are not statistics. These are our people.

What makes this crisis so insidious is the lie embedded within it: that burnout is a personal failure, a deficit of resilience in individuals who simply were not strong enough. This framing is both wrong and dangerous. Burnout is a systems problem dressed in the clothing of an individual disease. The hypothalamic-pituitary axis does not distinguish between moral failing and structural overload — it simply converts chronic stress into biological dysregulation. When a physician spends more time in an electronic medical record than at the bedside, when call schedules compress the margins of human recovery, when financial insecurity and medical-legal exposure stack upon one another — the system is doing this to us. Recognizing that truth is not weakness. It is the beginning of repair.

The book you hold is built on that recognition. It understands that the cure must be as multidimensional as the cause. Energy must be actively managed — through sleep, nutrition, movement, and the kind of intentional stillness that practices like meditation and journaling create. Identity must be reclaimed, rooted not in performance metrics but in meaning — in the Japanese concept of Ikigai, the intersection of what you love, what you are good at, what the world needs, and what sustains you. Boundaries must be set not as acts of selfishness, but as acts of precision: with patients, with staff, with family, and with the relentless demands of a system that will take everything you offer and then ask for more. And financial clarity — the kind that frees a physician from the invisible shackles of lifestyle debt and deferred planning — must be treated as a dimension of wellness, not an afterthought.

I think often of Diana Nyad, who at sixty-four years old swam 110 miles through open ocean from Havana to Key West — completing on her fifth attempt what she could not finish on her first four. The journey took fifty-three hours. She faced jellyfish, sharks, and the crushing monotony of dark water. What carried her was not simply physical conditioning. It was a refusal to accept the narrative that the attempt was finished. That is the posture this book invites you to inhabit: not the naive optimism that the sea will calm, but the trained resilience that knows how to swim regardless.

As Associate Dean for Faculty Development and Residency Program Director at Texas Tech University Health Sciences Center, I have seen firsthand what it costs when we neglect this work — and what becomes possible when we commit to it. The physicians who endure and flourish are not those who simply push harder. They are those who learn to build and protect the interior architecture of their lives: their energy, their identity, their purpose, their relationships, and their financial foundation. They are those who have the courage to ask for help before the breaking point, and the wisdom to recognize that self-preservation is not a luxury — it is a professional obligation.

The ancient admonition echoes still: Physician, heal thyself. This book is a worthy answer to that call. Read it not as a passive observer, but as a practitioner ready to apply its prescriptions to the most important patient in your care — yourself.

Izi Obokhare, M.D.

Professor of Minimally Invasive Laparoscopic and Robotic Surgery
General Surgery Residency Program Director
Associate Dean for Faculty Development
Texas Tech University Health Sciences Center, Amarillo

TABLE OF CONTENTS

EXPANDED EDITION

INTRODUCTION

FINDING BALANCE
IN THE OR AND BEYOND

*A guide written for the surgeon who gives
everything — and wonders what's left*

The operating room is a cathedral of precision. Every surgeon who walks through those double doors understands this implicitly — the weight of the gown, the snap of the gloves, the quiet authority that settles in when the first incision is made. It is a world built on competence, concentration, and control. And yet, for all of that mastery inside the OR, the world beyond those doors can feel staggering, chaotic, and quietly crushing.

This book was written for you. For the female surgeon who has built a career that commands respect in corridors that were not designed with her in mind. For the senior resident running on three hours of sleep and a protein bar. For the attending physician who has spent so long pouring herself into her patients, her trainees, her institution — that she has quietly, dangerously, forgotten to pour anything back into herself.

♦ Dr. Amara, General Surgery Attending | 9 Years Post-Residency

Dr. Amara is an elite laparoscopic surgeon at a Level I trauma center. On paper, she is thriving — a busy caseload, a faculty appointment, a family she adores. But lately, she arrives to rounds already tired. She snaps at residents over small errors. She sits in her car for ten minutes before walking into the hospital, just trying to find the will to move. She calls it 'just a rough patch.' Her colleagues call it Tuesday. But what she is actually experiencing has a name: burnout.

Burnout, or a complete and total draining of the mind, body, and emotions, is not a sign of weakness. In surgical culture, it is often mistaken for dedication — because the behaviors that drive burnout (overworking, self-sacrifice, never saying no) are the same behaviors that are rewarded, celebrated, and expected. This book will help you see the difference — and more importantly, help you escape it.

Whether you are a trainee in the thick of a brutal fellowship, a mid-career surgeon feeling quietly hollow behind your credentials, or a chief trying to lead a team while privately running on empty — there is a way through. And it begins with understanding what is happening.

CHAPTER ONE
UNDERSTANDING BURNOUT

*When the most disciplined professionals
in the world run out of fuel*

Burnout is defined as a state of total emotional, mental, and physical exhaustion that develops after prolonged, unmanaged stress. It happens when the demands of your life consistently outpace your capacity to rest, recover, or feel genuinely rewarded for your effort. In surgery, those conditions are not the exception — they are baked into the culture.

Understanding burnout is the first act of defense against it. The surgeon's life is structured, from the earliest days of medical school, around endurance. You learned to push through fatigue. You were praised for being the last one in the hospital. You internalized the message, quietly and thoroughly, that needing rest is a kind of failure. This is precisely why burnout can be so invisible to the people who most need to name it.

The Three Stages in a Surgeon's Life

Stage 1 — Exhaustion: You are tired in a way that a good night's sleep no longer fixes. You arrive to the hospital drained, and you leave more drained still. And yet, the OR schedule fills, the clinic overflows, and the notes pile up.

Stage 2 — Detachment: The cases that once lit you up begin to feel like transactions. You find yourself going through the motions during patient conversations. The resident who asks an eager question feels like an interruption rather than an opportunity.

Stage 3 — Loss of Effectiveness: You begin making errors you would never have made five years ago — not technical errors necessarily, but relational ones. Miscommunications. Missed nuances. A sense that your sharpest self has gone somewhere without leaving an address.

♦ Dr. Priya, Colorectal Surgery Fellow | Year Two

Dr. Priya entered fellowship as one of the top residents in her program — technically gifted, emotionally intelligent, deeply committed to her patients. Eighteen months in, she finds herself dreading the operating room for the first time in her career. She performs beautifully — her hands have not forgotten anything. But her heart is no longer in the room. She identifies this as a personal failing. She increases her hours. The exhaustion deepens. This is the burnout cycle doing exactly what it does: disguising itself as a motivation problem when it is, in fact, a recovery problem.

♦ Dr. Michelle, Breast Surgical Oncologist | Academic Medical Center

Dr. Michelle's day begins at 5:30 a.m. and rarely ends before 8:00 p.m. She is the only Black female surgeon in her division — a distinction that carries invisible weight. Every presentation, every consult, every interaction with administration carries an additional layer of scrutiny she navigates without complaint. She loves her work. And she is burning out from it. Burnout for her does not announce itself loudly. It whispers — in the headaches she dismisses, the joy she can no longer locate in a clean resection, the loneliness of being perpetually exceptional in rooms that never quite expected her.

> *"Burnout in surgery does not look like weakness. It looks like showing up every single day — and slowly becoming someone you no longer recognize."*

Robert Amajoyi, MD; Ebere Jill Azumah, MD MPH

CHAPTER TWO

BEYOND STRESS:
THE HIDDEN COST OF BURNOUT

What the body keeps when
the surgeon will not stop

In surgical training, we are taught to master the body — to work within it, repair it, and save it. And yet, the same rigor we apply to our patients, we rarely turn toward ourselves. Burnout is not simply feeling tired after a hard week. It is a systemic dismantling — physical, mental, emotional, relational — that happens when chronic, unaddressed stress is left to accumulate like unpaid debt.

Physical Costs

The surgeon's body is her most essential instrument. Burnout corrodes it. Chronic fatigue that no amount of sleep can fix. Persistent headaches that arrive before rounds and stay through clinic. A weakened immune system that turns every winter into a losing battle. Muscle tension that lives in the neck and shoulders — exactly where the hours of standing and operating have built their home. Hormonal disruption that can affect sleep cycles, reproductive health, and metabolic function. These are not inconveniences. They are warnings.

> ♦ **Dr. Kezia, Obstetric & Gynecologic Surgeon | Community Hospital**
>
> *Dr. Kezia had her third UTI of the year in October. She laughed it off — surgeons do not always have time to use the restroom during long cases, and hydration is often secondary to the case. What she did not laugh off, but also did not address, was the fatigue that made getting out of bed feel like wading through concrete. Her body was sending signals. Her training had taught her to override signals. Burnout had found the perfect hiding place.*

Mental and Cognitive Costs

The precision that surgery demands — the millimeter decisions, the ability to hold a mental map of anatomy while simultaneously managing a room — requires a mind that is sharp, rested, and clear. Burnout steals all three. Brain fog settles in. Decision fatigue arrives earlier in the day. Creativity — the kind that finds an elegant solution when the anatomy surprises you — begins to dim. The surgeon still performs, but she performs with less of herself in the room.

Emotional and Relational Costs

Compassion fatigue is not a character flaw — it is a physiological consequence of extended emotional labor without recovery. For a surgeon who spends her days holding space for frightened patients, grieving families, and overwhelmed trainees, this is not a distant theoretical risk. It is an occupational reality. When burnout deepens, she may find herself going emotionally numb in the clinic — not because she stopped caring, but because her capacity for care has been depleted without replenishment.

◆ Dr. Sandra, Pediatric Surgeon | Children's Hospital

Dr. Sandra has performed more than a thousand operations on children under the age of ten. She chose pediatric surgery because she could not imagine caring more about anything. Three years into her attending role, she notices that when a mother begins to cry in the pre-op bay, she no longer feels the instinctive swell of empathy that once moved her to reach for the woman's hand. She feels instead a hollow professionalism — competent, correct, and entirely disconnected. She is not a lesser surgeon. She is a burned-out one.

◆ Dr. Amara (continued) | Home

Her husband mentions, gently, that she has been absent even when she is present. That dinner conversations have become reporting sessions. That their children ask for her and she is technically there — phone down, eyes forward — but somehow still in the hospital. This is the relational cost of burnout: it does not stay inside the hospital walls. It travels home in the car with her, sits at the table, and quietly rearranges the architecture of her most important relationships.

> *"You cannot give from an empty vessel. The surgeon who saves others while quietly depleting herself has not escaped the patient role — she has merely postponed it."*

Robert Amajoyi, MD; Ebere Jill Azumah, MD MPH

CHAPTER THREE

THE SCIENCE OF BURNOUT: BRAIN, BODY, AND EMOTIONS

*What is happening beneath the surface
of the surgeon who cannot stop*

As surgeons and physicians, we respect mechanism. Understanding how burnout works at the neurological and physiological level is not merely academic — it is the foundation of a rational strategy to address it. You are not imagining the exhaustion. You are not simply 'stressed.' Your hypothalamic-pituitary-adrenal (HPA) axis is working exactly as designed — but in a context that was never designed for it.

Here is the mechanism: A stress trigger fires — an emergency case at 2 a.m., a complication on the floor, an unreasonable administrative demand, a microaggression in the attending lounge that you absorb and file away. Your hypothalamus signals the pituitary; cortisol and adrenaline flood the system. Heart rate climbs. Focus sharpens. In the short term, this is adaptive — it is what allows you to perform under pressure. But when the triggers are relentless and recovery is absent, the system does not reset. It stays switched on. And over time, it burns out.

What Chronic Stress Does to the Surgeon's Brain

▶ The prefrontal cortex weakens — the seat of judgment, patience, and logical reasoning. The surgeon who snaps at a circulating nurse is not rude; she is neurologically depleted.

▶ The amygdala becomes hyperactive — keeping her in a state of low-grade threat response. Small setbacks feel catastrophic. Normal friction feels personal.

▶ The hippocampus shrinks — making it harder to contextualize experience and form stable memories. The surgeon may find herself forgetting conversations, losing track of details she would once have held effortlessly.

▶ Neurotransmitter depletion sets in — serotonin, dopamine, norepinephrine all diminish under sustained stress. This produces the characteristic burnout signature: a hybrid of depression and anxiety that feels unlike either.

♦ Dr. Priya (continued) | Post-Call

After a 28-hour call shift, Dr. Priya sat in her car and could not remember whether she had signed the discharge paperwork on her patient in Room 14. She had — she always did. But her hippocampus, flooded with cortisol for the better part of a year, could no longer give her that certainty. She went back inside to check. She was correct. But the doubt — that creeping, unfamiliar self-distrust —

was new. And it frightened her more than any case she had faced in the OR.

♦ Dr. Michelle (continued) | Department Meeting

In a faculty meeting, a colleague dismissed Dr. Michelle's proposal for a new protocol with a wave of his hand. It was not the first time. In the past, she would have felt the sting, recalibrated, and returned with a stronger argument. Today, she felt nothing — a blankness where her professional fire used to live. Her amygdala, exhausted from years of navigating bias and overwork, had shifted from hypervigilance into the second phase of burnout: emotional shutdown. The numbness is not peace. It is depletion dressed as calm.

> *"The surgeon who 'just pushes through' is not stronger than the one who rests. She is simply borrowing against a neurological debt that will eventually come due."*

Robert Amajoyi, MD; Ebere Jill Azumah, MD MPH

CHAPTER FOUR

WHY BURNOUT IS MORE COMMON THAN YOU THINK

The epidemic hiding inside the most competent profession in the world

Ask any surgeon in any hospital in the country whether they know a colleague who has experienced burnout, and you will not find a single one who hesitates. The hand goes up immediately. The name comes readily. What takes longer — what often never arrives — is the moment the surgeon recognizes herself in that description.

Studies consistently show that physician burnout rates exceed fifty percent across specialties, with surgical fields among the highest. Female surgeons face compounded risk factors: gender bias, the invisible tax of performing competence in skeptical environments, the cultural expectation to be both exceptional professionally and seamlessly available personally. The burnout is not a reflection of inadequacy. It is a rational response to an irrational set of demands.

◆ Dr. Kezia (continued) | At a Colleague's Retirement Party

At the retirement dinner for a surgeon she admired, Dr. Kezia listened to speech after speech describing a woman who 'never complained,' who 'was always available,' who 'sacrificed everything for her patients and her program.' The room erupted in applause. Dr. Kezia applauded too. It was only on the drive home that she recognized the chill that had settled in her chest — the realization that the virtues being celebrated were the same behaviors that had ground this woman down for forty years. The culture was not celebrating a career. It was celebrating endurance. And calling it excellence.

◆ Dr. Amara (continued) | Peer Support Group

When Dr. Amara finally attended a physician wellness session at her institution — she went only because her department chief made attendance a quiet expectation — she sat in a room of eight surgeons. The facilitator asked who had felt detached from their work in the past six months. Seven of the eight hands went up. Dr. Amara was the eighth. She raised her hand thirty seconds later, after the silence made the truth unavoidable. The room did not fall apart. It held together better than it had in months, because finally, everyone was speaking the same language.

Burnout is common because the system that produces surgeons rewards the very behaviors that cause burnout. Recognizing this is not an indictment of medicine. It is the beginning of an honest conversation about what sustainable excellence actually requires.

Robert Amajoyi, MD; Ebere Jill Azumah, MD MPH

CHAPTER FIVE

13 SIGNS OF BURNOUT
— AND SPOTTING THEM EARLY

*The signals a surgeon is trained to
observe in others, turned inward*

A surgeon can read a patient's decline in the subtlest of signs — a shift in vitals, a change in affect, an intuition formed from thousands of hours of clinical observation. That same diagnostic precision, turned toward the self, can save a career. Here are the thirteen most common signs of burnout as they present in a surgical life.

1. You cannot muster the energy to care anymore.

The attending who once spent twenty minutes explaining a diagnosis now delivers it in three. Not because she has become unkind — but because her reservoir of engaged care has run dry. For Dr. Sandra, it was the moment she realized she no longer remembered her patients' names after discharge.

2. Emotional numbness or detachment.

Dr. Michelle noticed she was completing operative notes with clinical accuracy and zero emotional presence — as though she were documenting someone else's cases.

3. Tiredness that sleep cannot touch.

Dr. Priya slept nine hours on her day off and woke up exhausted. Not physically sore — she was used to that. Existentially drained, in a way that rest could not reach.

4. Persistent desire to isolate.

The female surgeon who once organized the departmental lunch now declines every invitation. Not because she dislikes her colleagues — because she has nothing left to bring to any room that isn't the OR.

5. Over-reliance on coping mechanisms.

Late-night wine to decompress. Skipping meals, then eating from vending machines. The coffee that started as one cup and became a continuous IV drip of function.

6. More mistakes than usual.

Not operative mistakes — the technical precision often holds longest. But forgotten callbacks. A missed note. A patient who fell through a gap in follow-up that she would never have allowed before.

7. A sense of not knowing yourself anymore.

Dr. Amara found herself sitting in her car after a successful case — one that would have thrilled her two years ago — feeling absolutely nothing. She did not recognize the emptiness as hers.

8. Your body is giving physical distress signals.

Recurring headaches, GI complaints, jaw tension from clenching through long cases. The body sends messages in the only language it has.

9. Loss of interest in what once brought joy.

Dr. Kezia used to run five miles three times a week. She stopped without deciding to.

10. Helplessness or hopelessness.

Not the clinical despair of depression — something quieter. A sense that the institutional problems are too large, that nothing she does changes anything, that she is very small inside a very indifferent machine.

11. Disordered sleep.

Too much on days off, too little on call nights — not because of the pager, but because the mind will not quiet.

12. Procrastination and task avoidance.

The inbox that goes unanswered for days. The paper that does not get submitted. The administrative task that gets moved to next week again and again.

13. Questioning whether the work matters.

This one is perhaps the most frightening for a surgeon — because she chose this path from a place of profound purpose. When that purpose becomes inaccessible, it does not mean it is gone. It means burnout has put it behind a wall.

CHAPTER SIX

WHY WE BURN OUT IN OUR MODERN LIVES

*The architecture of a profession
designed to push beyond human limits*

Burnout does not arrive from a single catastrophic event. It is built, incrementally, from the accumulated weight of structural demands that exceed the human body's capacity for sustained performance without recovery. For the surgeon, those demands are not theoretical — they are written into the schedule, the culture, the very language of excellence.

Work-Related Causes

The OR schedule that runs until 9 p.m. The department meeting scheduled at 7 a.m. The performance metrics that measure output without accounting for the human cost of producing it. The double standard — documented, persistent, infuriating — whereby a female surgeon who advocates for herself is labeled 'difficult,' while the same behavior in her male counterpart is called 'leadership.' Unrealistic expectations, lack of recognition, and misaligned institutional values do not merely cause frustration. They cause burnout.

◆ Dr. Michelle (continued) | Promotion Cycle

Dr. Michelle applied for a division chief position she had earned three times over — by publication record, clinical volume, and the quiet, constant excellence of her work. The position went to a male colleague with a shorter curriculum vitae and a louder presence in the administrative hallways. No one said the word 'discrimination.' No one needed to. Dr. Michelle returned to the OR the next morning and did her job brilliantly. And the invisible weight she had been carrying — the weight of knowing that excellence alone would not be sufficient — grew heavier.

Personal and Lifestyle Causes

The surgeon who is also a mother carries a load that the institutional calendar was not designed to accommodate. School pickup at 3:30 p.m. conflicts with the afternoon clinic that runs to 5:00. Weekend call conflicts with the Saturday soccer game that her child has mentioned four times this week. These are not small frictions. They are daily arithmetic in which something — usually her — does not add up.

◆ Dr. Sandra (continued) | On Parental Leave

Dr. Sandra returned from twelve weeks of maternity leave to discover that her OR block time had been reallocated in her absence. She was told it was 'temporary.' It was not. The negotiation to reclaim it took six months — six months in which she also managed a newborn, a breast pump in the call room, and the silent calculus of wondering whether

her colleagues would have faced the same outcome. They would not. She knew this. She said nothing, and carried more.

Inner and Psychological Causes

Perfectionism is the shadow side of the surgical temperament. The same drive for precision that makes a great surgeon also makes her exquisitely vulnerable to burnout — because perfection, by definition, is never achieved. She will always find the thing that could have been better, the outcome that was not what she wanted, the trainee she did not reach quite the way she intended. Without the counterbalance of self-compassion, perfectionism becomes a loop with no exit.

◆ Dr. Priya (continued) | After a Complication

Dr. Priya's patient developed a post-operative leak. It was caught early, managed correctly, and the patient recovered fully. By every objective measure, she had done everything right — including recognizing the complication before it became a crisis. But she replayed it for eleven days. She reviewed the operative video four times. She arrived at the same conclusion each time — technically, she had done nothing wrong — and felt no relief. Perfectionism does not respond to evidence. It responds to rest, compassion, and community. None of those had been part of Dr. Priya's prescription for herself.

Robert Amajoyi, MD; Ebere Jill Azumah, MD MPH

CHAPTER SEVEN

BREAKING FREE FROM THE CYCLE

*Understanding the loop before you
can step outside it*

Burnout is not a single event — it is a cycle. And like any cycle, it perpetuates itself by creating conditions that make the next rotation more likely than the last. For the surgeon who operates inside a culture that rewards overwork and stigmatizes vulnerability, the cycle can spin for years before it is named for what it is.

Step 1: Overcommitment

The case load grows because she is excellent and everyone knows it. She agrees to the committee because no one else will step up. She stays late because the resident needs supervision and she will not cut corners on education. Each decision is individually defensible. Cumulatively, they are unsustainable.

Step 2: Stress builds

The long hours begin cannibalizing sleep. The paperwork bleeds into evenings that were supposed to be for her family. Self-care — the run, the meal cooked at home, the hour of reading — disappears first because it feels most negotiable.

Step 3: Exhaustion

She arrives to early rounds already running a deficit. She compensates with caffeine, discipline, and the sheer force of professional identity. The performance holds. The person behind it is fraying.

Step 4: Detachment

The cases that once lit her up become routine. The resident who needs extra teaching becomes a burden she silently resents — and then resents herself for resenting.

Step 5: Crisis or collapse

It may be physical — the illness that finally sidelines her. It may be relational — the conversation with her partner that cannot be avoided any longer. It may be professional — the outburst in the OR that she cannot walk back. Something breaks the surface.

Step 6: Temporary relief

A few days off. A vacation that is mostly spent on email. A medication for the headaches. The acute pressure eases. She feels, briefly, like herself again.

Step 7: Return and repeat

She goes back. The schedule is waiting. The inbox is waiting. The culture is waiting. And without systemic change — in her structure, her mindset, or her boundaries — the cycle begins again, and usually accelerates.

♦ Dr. Amara (continued) | Recognizing the Loop

It was her third bout with the same cycle in four years when Dr. Amara finally sat with her journal and mapped it out — not the incidents, but the pattern. She could see it clearly once she stopped looking at each episode in isolation. The overcommitment. The exhaustion. The brief recovery. The return to the same conditions that had created the burnout in the first place. She had been treating the symptoms. She had never addressed the structure. That morning, she started.

> *"You cannot rest your way out of a system problem. But you cannot fix the system until you have rested enough to think clearly about what needs to change."*

Robert Amajoyi, MD; Ebere Jill Azumah, MD MPH

CHAPTER EIGHT

THE MINDSET SHIFT: PERMISSION TO REST

*The most radical thing a surgeon
can prescribe for herself*

In the surgical culture, rest is frequently experienced as transgression. The surgeon who leaves at 5:00 p.m. when her work is done may feel a pull of guilt as she walks past colleagues who are still at their desks. The attending who takes a full lunch break without charting may wonder if she is being perceived as lazy. This is not weakness. This is indoctrination — and it is slowly killing excellent physicians.

The foundational mindset shift required to escape burnout is this: rest is not a reward for completed work. It is a precondition for doing the work at all. For the surgeon, this reframe is not merely philosophical — it is clinical. A rested surgeon is a safer surgeon. A recovered physician makes better decisions. Self-care is not selfishness. It is the standard of care applied to the most important instrument in the room: you.

♦ Dr. Kezia (continued) | A Turning Point

Her mentor — a retired cardiothoracic surgeon of thirty-five years — told her something she has never forgotten: 'Kezia, the hospital will always need one more hour of you. The hospital does not know when to stop. That is your job — to know.' She had heard it as advice then. Standing in her kitchen at 10 p.m., exhausted and eating cereal for the third consecutive night, she heard it as a prescription.

Permission Statements for the Surgeon's Life

If the internal voice of burnout sounds like a demanding attending who never approves of your performance, you are allowed to replace it. Deliberately. Repeatedly. These permission statements are not affirmations — they are clinical reframes:

- ▶ Leaving on time is not abandonment. It is professional sustainability.

- ▶ Resting does not make me a lesser surgeon. It makes me a safer one.

- ▶ I am allowed to have a life outside of this hospital.

- ▶ My needs are not an inconvenience. They are the infrastructure that makes everything else possible.

- ▶ Protecting my energy is not weakness. It is clinical leadership.

◆ Dr. Sandra (continued) | Scheduling Rest

Dr. Sandra began treating her Thursday evenings the same way she treated her OR block: non-negotiable, protected, and unavailable for reallocation. She told her chief she had 'a standing commitment.' She did. It was to herself. She used the time to run, to read to her children, to cook a meal that took longer than twenty minutes. Three months later, her resident evaluations — which had quietly declined over the previous year — began to recover. The best thing she did for her trainees was protect one evening a week for herself.

Robert Amajoyi, MD; Ebere Jill Azumah, MD MPH

34

CHAPTER NINE

STRESS MANAGEMENT TOOLS FOR DAILY LIFE

Strategies that work in the gaps between cases

The surgeon's schedule does not always allow for a forty-minute yoga class between the morning's laparoscopic cases and the afternoon's clinic. Stress management for the surgical life must be practical, portable, and effective in the margins. These are tools that work in the world you actually inhabit — not the one a wellness influencer imagines.

Body-Based Strategies

♦ Dr. Priya (continued) | Between Cases

Between her second and third case, with twenty minutes on the clock, Dr. Priya began a practice she calls 'the reset.' She walks to the end of the hallway, away from the surgical suite noise, and practices box breathing for four minutes: inhale four counts, hold four, exhale four, hold four. She returns to the room physically different — her heart rate lower, her prefrontal cortex back online. She once dismissed breathing exercises as non-clinical. She now prescribes them to her residents.

▶ Box breathing (4-4-4-4): four counts in, four hold, four out, four hold. Do this for four minutes between cases.

▶ Progressive muscle relaxation: from scalp to feet, tense and release each group. Particularly valuable before a difficult conversation.

▶ Movement micro-breaks: three minutes of walking the corridor changes the neurochemical environment more than most people realize.

▶ The 5-4-3-2-1 grounding method: name five things you see, four you feel, three you hear, two you smell, one you taste. Interrupts spiral thinking instantly.

Mind-Based Strategies

◆ Dr. Michelle (continued) | The Worry Window

Dr. Michelle began setting a ten-minute worry window each evening — a deliberate, timed period in which she allowed herself to ruminate on the day's frustrations. When the timer rang, she closed the notebook and switched to something that required her physical engagement: a walk, dinner preparation, her daughter's homework. The worry did not disappear — but it stopped spreading. Contained, it became manageable. Uncontained, it had been consuming her evenings entirely.

- ▶ Journaling: not journaling about events, but about feelings — the ones you have no time to process during the day.

- ▶ The worry window: ten minutes of designated overthinking, then a deliberate redirect.

- ▶ Reframing stress as signal, not threat: 'What is this feeling telling me about what I need?'

Lifestyle-Based Strategies

Sleep, nutrition, and movement are not self-indulgences for the surgeon — they are clinical infrastructure. The surgeon who is nutritionally depleted, sleep-deprived, and sedentary is operating at a measurable deficit. These are not lifestyle choices. They are professional responsibilities.

Robert Amajoyi, MD; Ebere Jill Azumah, MD MPH

CHAPTER TEN

THE ROLE OF SLEEP, NUTRITION, AND MOVEMENT

The trilogy that the OR depends on —
and that the surgeon often withholds from herself

You would not operate on a patient who had not slept in thirty hours. You would not ask a resident to make consequential decisions when their blood sugar has been running on a granola bar since 5 a.m. And yet, the surgeon applies to herself a standard of care she would never prescribe to anyone else. The three pillars of physical recovery — sleep, nutrition, and movement — are not luxuries. They are the foundation upon which surgical excellence is actually built.

Sleep

Sleep is the body's only truly restorative state. During deep sleep, cortisol levels fall, cellular repair occurs, memories consolidate, and the emotional processing that daytime does not allow finds its way through. For the surgeon who averages five hours on call nights and six on recovery days, this process is chronically interrupted — and the cumulative deficit is physiologically real.

◆ Dr. Amara (continued) | The Sleep Experiment

Dr. Amara made one change for thirty days: she committed to seven hours of sleep on every non-call night, regardless of what remained undone. The first week was uncomfortable — the guilt of an unfinished inbox, the anxiety of leaving things in a state of incompletion. By week three, she noticed her concentration had sharpened noticeably. By week four, her husband said, quietly, 'You're back.' She had not known she had left.

Nutrition

The surgeon who skips breakfast, eats lunch at 3 p.m. from a vending machine, and arrives home too tired to cook is not being disciplined — she is being harmed by a culture that treats eating as optional when the schedule is full. Sustained blood glucose levels are directly tied to decision-making quality, emotional regulation, and cognitive endurance. The meal is not a reward for a completed clinic. It is a prerequisite for running one well.

Movement

Exercise is not about aesthetics for the surgeon — it is about neurological regulation. Physical movement is one of the most evidence-based interventions for cortisol reduction, dopamine replenishment, and the disruption of the stress cycle. Thirty minutes of intentional movement — walking, yoga, running, swimming — produces changes in the brain that medication can approximate but not replicate.

♦ Dr. Kezia (continued) | Movement as Medicine

Dr. Kezia could not commit to a gym membership she would not keep. So she made a smaller promise: every day, regardless of the shift, she would walk for twenty minutes before entering the hospital or after leaving it. Not for fitness. Not to train for anything. Simply as a daily act of transition — from surgeon to person, or from person back to surgeon. Six months later, she told her therapist it was the single most effective intervention she had tried. It cost nothing. It returned everything.

Robert Amajoyi, MD; Ebere Jill Azumah, MD MPH

CHAPTER ELEVEN

REBUILDING MENTAL WELLNESS

*The slow, non-linear, deeply worthwhile
work of returning to yourself*

Mental wellness, for the surgeon, is not a destination she reaches once and then maintains effortlessly. It is a practice — an ongoing engagement with her own inner life that requires the same consistency she brings to her clinical skills. Rebuilding it after burnout is not a linear process. There will be good weeks and difficult ones. The goal is not perfection. It is direction.

Inner Practices

◆ Dr. Sandra (continued) | The Gratitude Experiment

On the advice of a therapist she initially dismissed as 'soft,' Dr. Sandra began writing three sentences at the end of each shift — not about what had gone well clinically, but about what had moved her. A parent's relief. A resident's breakthrough. The way afternoon light came through the window of the PICU waiting room. She felt silly for the first two weeks. By the end of the month, she was noticing things again. Burnout had made her blind to anything that was not a problem. Gratitude gave her eyes back.

▶ Journaling feelings, not just events — the emotional processing that the OR does not allow.

▶ Positive self-talk: replacing the inner critic's voice with the voice of a trusted mentor.

▶ Mindfulness: noticing what is happening without immediately categorizing it as good or bad.

▶ Daily gratitude: three specific observations, written at the end of the shift.

Relational Practices

Isolation is both a symptom of burnout and an accelerant. The surgeon who withdraws from connection because she has nothing left to give is also withdrawing from the very resource that most effectively replenishes her. Rebuilding relational practices is not about adding another obligation. It is about allowing herself to receive.

♦ Dr. Michelle (continued) | The Peer Group

Dr. Michelle joined a small peer support group of six female surgeons — three from her institution, three from neighboring hospitals. They met by video every other Thursday for an hour. No agenda. No presentations. No performance. Just six women who understood exactly what the other was navigating, without needing it explained. She has not missed a session in a year. She says it is the most honest hour of her month.

Robert Amajoyi, MD; Ebere Jill Azumah, MD MPH

CHAPTER TWELVE

BOUNDARIES THAT PROTECT YOUR ENERGY

*The skill they did not teach in residency —
and the one that will save your career*

Boundaries are not walls. They are the clearly defined edges of a territory that you are responsible for protecting — and no one in your professional ecosystem will protect it as consistently, or as necessarily, as you will. For the female surgeon who has spent her career navigating environments where her presence is already a negotiation, learning to set and hold boundaries is not merely personal development. It is professional survival.

Professional Boundaries

♦ Dr. Priya (continued) | The After-Hours Text

When her program director began texting after 9 p.m. with administrative questions that were not clinically urgent,

Dr. Priya struggled for three months before she said anything. When she finally did — calmly, professionally, with clear language: 'I am not able to respond to non-urgent messages after 9 p.m.; I will address them first thing in the morning' — she waited for the fallout. There was none. Her director said, 'Fair enough.' The texts stopped. She had spent three months afraid of a ten-second conversation.

▶ Time cutoffs: define your availability window and communicate it explicitly.

▶ Protected breaks: block them on the calendar. Treat them as OR time.

▶ Workload limits: 'I can take this on, but I will need to adjust my other priorities first' is a complete, professional sentence.

Relational Boundaries

◆ Dr. Amara (continued) | At Home

Dr. Amara and her husband established a rule: the first thirty minutes after she arrived home were hers — a decompression window in which she was neither on call nor on duty as a mother, wife, or planner of family logistics. She changed clothes, she walked outside briefly, she was simply a person for half an hour. This boundary was not selfish. It was the thing that made her actually present for the next four hours of family life, instead of physically there and emotionally somewhere else.

Mental and Emotional Boundaries

▶ The self-talk filter: 'Getting this done is better than getting it perfect.'

▶ Unfollowing accounts that provoke comparison rather than inspiration.

▶ The worry window: ten minutes of permitted rumination, then a hard redirect.

▶ An information diet: curating the news and social media that enters your nervous system each day.

◆ Dr. Sandra (continued) | Saying No

When the department chair asked Dr. Sandra to join her fourth committee of the academic year, she said something she had never said before: 'I am at capacity right now. I would not be able to contribute the way this work deserves. I need to decline.' She did not apologize. She did not over-explain. She felt her heart rate climb when she sent the email, and she sent it anyway. The chair responded with respect. The boundary held. She learned something she should have been taught in her intern year: 'No' is a complete sentence, and it is sometimes the most professional thing she can say.

Robert Amajoyi, MD; Ebere Jill Azumah, MD MPH

CHAPTER THIRTEEN

RECONNECTING WITH JOY AND MEANING

*Recovering what burnout buried —
and discovering it is still there*

One of the cruelest aspects of burnout is the way it severs the surgeon from the very thing that brought her to surgery in the first place. The purpose — the bone-deep certainty that this work matters — does not disappear. It becomes inaccessible, buried under the weight of exhaustion and detachment. Reconnecting with it is not about manufacturing enthusiasm. It is about creating the conditions in which what was always there can surface again.

Start with Small, Joyful Moments

♦ Dr. Kezia (continued) | The Joy Journal

Dr. Kezia's therapist suggested she keep a joy journal — not a gratitude journal, not a productivity tracker, but a record of the moments in each day that made something inside her feel lighter. At first her entries were thin: the first coffee of the morning. A patient who made her laugh. The drive home with the windows down. Over months, the entries lengthened. She began to notice that joy had not left her life. It had been drowned out. The journal gave it a frequency she could hear again.

Reconnect with Core Values

Ask yourself: Why did I choose surgery? Not the answer you give at grand rounds — the real one, the one you told yourself at 2 a.m. during your second year of medical school when you were exhausted and uncertain and still, somehow, certain that this was the thing. That answer is still true. Burnout has not changed it. It has only temporarily made it inaudible.

♦ Dr. Michelle (continued) | Finding Her Why Again

Dr. Michelle had not thought about why she chose surgery in years — she had been too busy doing it. At the suggestion of a mentor, she wrote the story of the patient who made her want to be a surgeon. A woman named Dolores. Breast cancer, age forty-two, two daughters. Operated on by a team that was precise and cold. Dr. Michelle had been a third-year medical student observing, and she had held the woman's hand in pre-op and seen what that meant. She had decided then. Writing the story did not fix her burnout. But it reminded her who she was before it arrived. That was enough to begin.

Rediscover Creativity and Play

♦ Dr. Priya (continued) | Pottery

Dr. Priya started a beginner's pottery class because her neighbor mentioned it offhandedly and she had nothing to lose. She was terrible at it. The clay collapsed. The bowls were lopsided. She laughed — genuinely, out loud — for the first time in months. There was no performance metric. There was no evaluation. There was just her hands in the clay and the reminder that she was a person before she was a surgeon. She still goes every Thursday.

Robert Amajoyi, MD; Ebere Jill Azumah, MD MPH

54

CHAPTER FOURTEEN

DESIGNING A SUSTAINABLE FUTURE

Building a life that is built to last —
not just to endure

Sustainability is not a concept that belongs only to environmental science. It is the most important professional and personal question a surgeon can ask: Can I do this well, for a long time, without destroying myself in the process? The answer, historically, has too often been no. This chapter is about changing that answer — not by lowering the standard of surgical excellence, but by raising the standard of care applied to the surgeon herself.

The Burnout-Proof Lifestyle

A strong support system

Not the isolation of excellence, but the community of excellence — colleagues who know what the work costs, and who show up for each other.

Healthy, enforced boundaries

Not occasional limits, but structural protection of time, energy, and personal life — applied consistently, regardless of institutional pressure.

Protected rest

Scheduled, non-negotiable, and free of guilt. The surgeon who rests is not less dedicated. She is more sustainable.

Work-life balance as a design problem

Not a feeling to be achieved, but a structure to be built — intentionally, with specific decisions about time, availability, and priority.

Wellbeing as an ongoing practice

Not a one-time fix after a crisis, but a daily act of professional maintenance — as non-negotiable as sterilization technique.

◆ Dr. Amara (continued) | Designing Forward

Dr. Amara spent a weekend with a journal and a calendar. She mapped the previous year's burnout cycle, identified the three structural factors that perpetuated it — overcommitment to committees, absence of protected personal time, and a habit of responding to all messages regardless of urgency — and she changed each one. Not dramatically. Incrementally. One boundary at a time. A year later, she has not returned to the crisis stage of the cycle. She has not been perfect. But she has been directional. And in surgery, directional is everything.

CHAPTER FIFTEEN

THE ROLE OF COMMUNITY AND SUPPORT SYSTEMS

The thing that keeps the surgeon from disappearing into her own excellence

Surgery can be a solitary profession despite being practiced in rooms full of people. The surgeon is the apex of the hierarchy — which means she often has no one above her to whom she can say 'I am struggling.' She may have colleagues all around her and feel entirely alone. This is not a character flaw. It is an architectural problem with a structural solution: intentional community.

A genuine support system does more than provide emotional comfort. It redistributes cognitive load. It offers perspective when burnout narrows vision to a tunnel. It catches the surgeon before she reaches the crisis stage — because the people who know her well are often the first to see that she has begun to disappear.

◆ Dr. Sandra (continued) | The Mentor Who Noticed

It was her surgical mentor — a woman twenty years her senior — who said, during a routine coffee meeting, 'You don't laugh the same way you used to.' Not a dramatic intervention. Not a crisis conversation. Just a woman who knew her well enough to notice a subtle change in the quality of her joy. That sentence opened a three-hour conversation that Dr. Sandra has called, in retrospect, the turning point. She had not known how much she needed to be seen until someone finally saw her.

◆ Dr. Michelle (continued) | Finding Her Community

Dr. Michelle eventually found her community not inside her institution but outside it — a national organization of Black female surgeons who gathered twice a year and connected monthly by video. What she found there was not mentorship in the traditional sense. It was recognition. The particular exhaustion of navigating excellence in environments built for someone else — that exhaustion had a name, and twenty other women in the room shared it. She stopped feeling like a problem unique to herself. She started feeling like a person inside a story that was larger than her own.

Find your people. Cultivate the relationships that restore rather than drain. Seek the mentor who will tell you the truth. Join the group where you do not have to perform. These connections are not optional extras appended to a surgical career. They are the infrastructure that sustains one.

CHAPTER SIXTEEN

THRIVING, NOT JUST SURVIVING

The life beyond endurance — and how to build it

There is a version of the surgical career that is built entirely on endurance. Get through the case. Get through the shift. Get through the year. This version is recognizable. It is also insufficient. Not because it fails to produce excellent surgeons — it often does — but because it produces them at a cost that is never accounted for in the curriculum vitae or the departmental dashboard.

Thriving looks different. It looks like energy that does not require caffeine as a prerequisite. It looks like choosing a difficult case with something that resembles enthusiasm. It looks like being present at the dinner table without part of the mind still in the hospital. It looks like a resident who asks a question and sees, in her attending's face, that she is genuinely welcomed. It looks like a surgeon who has made her peace with the fact that the work is demanding and the life is worth living.

♦ Dr. Priya (continued) | Two Years Later

Two years after the burnout that nearly ended her fellowship, Dr. Priya accepted an attending position at an academic center. In her first faculty meeting, a senior colleague asked her what her greatest professional strength was. She thought for a moment and said: 'I know what I need to keep going. And I have learned that knowing that is not a liability — it is a clinical skill.' The room was quiet for a moment. Then the department chief nodded. 'That,' she said, 'is what we need more of here.'

♦ Dr. Amara (continued) | The Life She Designed

Dr. Amara still works hard. She still answers difficult calls at 2 a.m. She still carries the weight of a division and the futures of the trainees who look to her. But she also runs three mornings a week. She eats lunch most days. She protects Sunday evenings as if they were OR block time. Her children know her laugh again. Her husband said last month that she seemed lighter. She did not argue with him. She had worked very hard to become that.

> *"Thriving is not the absence of difficulty. It is the presence of yourself, fully and sustainably, inside the life you have chosen — not despite the demands, but equipped for them."*

CONCLUSION

FINAL THOUGHTS

A letter to the surgeon who has read this far

If you have read this far, something in these pages has found you. Perhaps you recognized yourself in Dr. Amara, sitting in her car before rounds. Perhaps you saw Dr. Priya's perfectionism, or Dr. Michelle's invisible weight, or Dr. Sandra's compassion fatigue, or Dr. Kezia's body quietly keeping score while her mind insisted everything was fine. You are not alone in what you are carrying. You are in the company of some of the most talented, dedicated, and quietly exhausted people in the world.

Burnout is not a permanent state. It is not a sentence. It is not evidence of inadequacy or weakness or the wrong choice of career. It is what happens when a brilliant, driven person gives and gives and gives without a system — internal or institutional — that allows her to receive.

The work of recovery is incremental. One permission statement. One protected evening. One honest conversation with a mentor. One boundary held. One morning where you eat breakfast before you look at your phone. These are not small things. They are the architecture of a sustainable career — built one deliberate choice at a time.

You became a surgeon because something in you knew that this was the work you were made for. That knowing has not left you. It is waiting for you on the other side of the recovery you have been postponing.

Rest. Return to yourself. And then return to the OR — not as the surgeon who survived burnout, but as the surgeon who learned what she needed to truly thrive.

> *"The operating room will always need you. Make sure you are actually there — not just your hands, but all of you."*

— With deep respect, for every surgeon who dares to ask for more than endurance —

EXPANDED EDITION

*Deep dives, research, reflection prompts,
and expanded surgeon narratives*

Robert Amajoyi, MD; Ebere Jill Azumah, MD MPH

INTRODUCTION – EXPANDED

FINDING BALANCE IN THE OR AND BEYOND

A deeper look at the world that created this crisis — and the path out of it

Before we begin the work of this book, let us take a moment to name what is true: the surgical profession, at its best, is one of the most extraordinary vocations a human being can pursue. To hold in your hands the power to remove a cancer, to repair a bowel, to restore function to a body in crisis — this is not merely a job. It is a calling. And for the surgeon reading these words, it is almost certainly the thing that has organized her entire adult life — her education, her relationships, her sense of self, her very identity.

That is precisely what makes burnout in surgery so insidious, and so devastating. Because burnout does not attack something peripheral. It attacks the center. It reaches into the place where purpose lives and drains it quietly, systematically, and often invisibly — until the surgeon wakes one morning and cannot locate the reason she chose this life in the first place.

This book was born from a recognition that the existing conversation about physician wellness too often speaks in generalities. It offers breathing exercises to people who can barely find two minutes between cases. It recommends meditation to individuals who have been awake for twenty hours. It speaks of 'work-life balance' to surgeons who know, from lived experience, that the pager does not respect the concept of balance. What was needed was something different: a resource that speaks the specific language of the surgical life, that understands the culture from the inside, and that offers strategies built for the world surgeons actually inhabit — not the one that wellness marketing imagines.

Who This Book Is For

This book is for the female surgeon who has spent her career building excellence in environments that were not built for her. It is for the resident who is brilliant and exhausted in equal measure and has not yet learned that those two things are not supposed to coexist permanently. It is for the attending who has achieved everything she set out to achieve and finds, quietly and inexplicably, that achievement no longer feels like enough. It is for the program director who pours herself into her trainees and has no one pouring back. It is for the surgeon of color who carries the additional weight of navigating bias alongside the ordinary weight of surgical culture — and who has been told, implicitly or explicitly, that naming that weight is itself a form of weakness.

It is also for the male surgeon who recognizes in these pages something he has felt but not named. The burnout cycle does not discriminate by gender — though its contributing factors are not distributed equally. The structural barriers, the invisible taxes, the compounding demands of caregiving and professional performance that fall disproportionately on women in surgery — these are real, and this book names them clearly. But the experience of depletion, detachment, and loss of purpose is a human experience. Any surgeon, of any background, who finds themselves in its grip will find something useful here.

How to Use This Book

This book is organized to move you from understanding through action. The early chapters build a clinical and scientific foundation — because surgeons, by nature, trust evidence. You will not be asked to adopt strategies you cannot understand mechanistically. The middle chapters offer tools — practical, portable, and designed for the margins of a surgical schedule. The later chapters turn toward the larger architecture: how to design a sustainable career, build a community, and move from surviving to genuinely thriving.

At the end of each chapter, you will find a Reflection and Journaling section. These prompts are not optional extras — they are the conversion mechanism that transforms intellectual understanding into lived change. The surgeon who reads but does not reflect may find herself informed but not transformed. The prompts take between five and fifteen minutes. They can be completed at the end of a shift, on a Sunday morning, or in the car before walking into the hospital. They are designed for your actual life.

You will also meet four surgeons throughout this book — Dr. Amara, Dr. Priya, Dr. Michelle, and Dr. Sandra — along with

Dr. Kezia. Their stories are composites, drawn from the real experiences of surgeons at every stage of their careers. They are not cautionary tales. They are portraits of excellence meeting its human limits — and finding a way through.

> *"You did not become a surgeon to merely endure. You became one to heal — and that begins with healing yourself."*

✏ Reflection & Journaling Prompts

1. *When was the last time you felt genuinely excited to go to work? What was happening in your life at that time that you are not experiencing now?*

2. *What does 'success' mean to you today — and how does that definition differ from the one you held when you first entered medicine?*

3. *If a beloved colleague described to you the symptoms you have been experiencing, what would you tell her? Write that advice as a letter to yourself.*

4. *What is the story you have been telling yourself about why you cannot rest? Where did that story come from?*

5. *Name one person in your life who knows the full weight of what you are carrying right now. If that person does not exist, what would it mean to create that relationship?*

CHAPTER ONE – EXPANDED

UNDERSTANDING BURNOUT

The clinical, cultural, and personal dimensions of a surgical epidemic

The word 'burnout' was introduced into the medical literature by psychologist Herbert Freudenberger in 1974, who used it to describe the exhaustion he observed in volunteer workers at a free clinic in New York City. He described people who had entered the work with enormous idealism and energy, and who had, over time, become depleted, cynical, and ineffective — not because they had stopped caring, but because caring, without adequate recovery, had cost them everything they had. The description is fifty years old. It reads like it was written yesterday, for surgery specifically.

In 2019, the World Health Organization formally classified burnout as an occupational phenomenon in the International Classification of Diseases (ICD-11), defining it as a syndrome resulting from chronic workplace stress that has not been successfully managed. Three dimensions characterize it: feelings of energy depletion or exhaustion; increased mental distance from one's job, or feelings of negativism or cynicism related to one's job; and reduced professional efficacy. These three dimensions map precisely onto the three stages described in the previous section of this book — exhaustion, detachment, and loss of effectiveness.

★ Research Spotlight: The Surgeon Burnout Epidemic

A 2020 survey of more than 7,000 surgeons published in the Journal of the American College of Surgeons found that 38.5% of surgeons reported significant burnout — a figure that many researchers believe underestimates the true prevalence due to underreporting driven by stigma. Female surgeons reported burnout at higher rates than their male counterparts (40.8% vs. 36.3%), with work-home conflict, harassment, and gender discrimination identified as significant contributing factors. A separate study from the Annals of Surgery found that nearly one in five surgeons had experienced suicidal ideation in the preceding year. These are not outliers. This is the landscape.

The Surgical Identity Problem

Surgery does not simply produce burnout — it creates conditions that make burnout almost structurally inevitable, and then trains its practitioners to be ashamed of experiencing it. From the first days of surgical training, the message is clear: the good surgeon pushes through. The good surgeon does not need to leave early. The good surgeon does not ask for help. The good surgeon performs, under any conditions, at the highest possible level. This is not malice — it is culture. And like all culture, it was transmitted from one generation to the next so smoothly and completely that it became invisible.

The surgical identity — the sense of self built upon competence, discipline, and service — is one of the most powerful professional identities in the world. It is also, unchecked, one of the most dangerous. When identity and performance become inseparable, any decline in performance becomes a threat not merely to the career but to the self. The surgeon who begins to slip — who makes more mistakes, who cares less, who cannot find the motivation to chart — is not just experiencing burnout. She is experiencing an existential crisis dressed in scrubs.

◆ Dr. Amara | The Identity Fracture

Dr. Amara had been described, since her intern year, as 'the one who never burns out.' It was meant as a compliment — a recognition of her extraordinary resilience. She wore it like a badge. By her ninth year of attending practice, she understood that the badge had become a prison. Because if Dr. Amara never burned out, then what she was experiencing — the fatigue, the numbness, the quiet dread — could not be burnout. It must be weakness. It must be a personal failing. It was, in fact, exactly what it looked like. But her identity had given her no language for it, and no permission to name it.

Burnout Versus Depression: Understanding the Distinction

One of the most important clinical distinctions to understand is the difference between burnout and clinical depression. They share many features — fatigue, loss of pleasure, emotional flatness, withdrawal — which is why they are so often confused. But they are not the same condition, and treating one as though it were the other leads to inadequate care.

Burnout is context-specific. The surgeon experiencing burnout typically feels relief on weekends, vacations, or days away from the hospital. She may find genuine joy outside of work — with her children, in her hobbies, in relationships — even as she dreads returning to the OR. Depression is pervasive. It follows the person regardless of context. The woman who feels as empty on Saturday morning as she does on Monday before rounds may be experiencing something that requires clinical intervention beyond lifestyle and boundary work.

This distinction matters for treatment. Burnout responds to structural changes: reduced workload, improved boundaries, enhanced recovery time, community, and meaning-making. Depression responds to clinical treatment: therapy, medication, structured support. Many surgeons experiencing burnout also develop secondary depression — which is why screening for both, and seeking appropriate professional help, is not optional. It is the standard of care applied to the self.

★ Research Spotlight: When Burnout Becomes Depression

Research published in Occupational and Environmental Medicine found that sustained occupational burnout significantly increases the risk of developing major depressive disorder. The pathway is neurobiological: chronic cortisol elevation disrupts serotonin and dopamine systems in ways that eventually produce clinical depression independent of workplace factors. This means that the surgeon who waits too long to address burnout may find, six months later, that structural changes alone are insufficient — that the brain chemistry has shifted in ways that require clinical support to repair. Early intervention is not optional. It is protective.

◆ Dr. Michelle | When the Weekends Stopped Helping

For three years, Dr. Michelle's weekends were her refuge. She cooked elaborate meals. She took her daughter to the farmers market. She felt, on Saturday mornings, like a person rather than a surgeon. Then, gradually, the weekends began to feel like the same shade of gray as the weekdays. The farmers market felt like an obligation. The cooking felt effortful. She could not identify a single moment in a given week that felt genuinely light. She called her internist. Her PHQ-9 score was 14. She started therapy. She also started the structural changes this book describes. Both were necessary. Neither alone would have been sufficient.

The Three Stages in Detail

The three stages of burnout — exhaustion, detachment, and loss of effectiveness — deserve more than a passing mention, because understanding which stage you are in is critical for determining what kind of intervention is most needed.

Stage One: Exhaustion. In this first stage, the person is still engaged — she still cares about her work, her patients, her trainees. But she is running on insufficient fuel. She compensates with caffeine, willpower, and professional identity. Her performance may still appear excellent to external observers. The warning signs are internal: the quality of sleep, the presence of chronic physical symptoms, the mental effort required to complete tasks that once felt automatic. This is the optimal stage for intervention — because the purpose is still accessible, and the structural changes required are not yet as extensive.

Stage Two: Detachment. By this stage, the emotional reserve has been significantly depleted. The surgeon begins to protect herself from further depletion by emotionally withdrawing from her work. The patients become cases. The residents become tasks. The relationships that once made the work meaningful become sources of obligation rather than connection. Cynicism develops — not because the person has become cynical by nature, but because cynicism is the mind's protective response to repeated disappointment. Intervention at this stage requires more significant change and more deliberate recovery.

Stage Three: Loss of Effectiveness. This is the stage of visible decline. Errors increase. Productivity falls. The professional identity — which was once such a driver of overperformance — begins to crack. The surgeon may consider leaving the profession entirely. She may become a liability to her team, not through lack of skill but through lack of presence. Recovery at this stage is possible, but it typically requires a significant life change — time away, professional help, and a fundamental restructuring of the conditions that produced the burnout.

♦ Dr. Priya | Mapping Her Own Stage

Dr. Priya had been telling herself she was in Stage One — just tired, just stressed, just needing a vacation — for eight months before she sat down with a piece of paper and listed what she actually felt. She had stopped enjoying the cases she once loved. She had started eating alone to avoid her fellow residents' questions. She had reviewed one of her operative videos three times not to improve her technique but to confirm she had not made an error she was afraid she had made. She was in Stage Two. The vacation she had been planning would not fix a Stage Two problem. She needed to understand that, and then she needed a different plan.

✐ Reflection & Journaling Prompts

1. *Based on the three stages described in this chapter, which stage most accurately describes where you are right now? What specific evidence from your life supports that assessment?*

2. *Describe your surgical identity in three sentences. Now describe who you are outside of that identity. If the second description is harder to write, what does that tell you?*

3. *Have you ever dismissed what you were experiencing*

as 'not real burnout' because you were still performing? What permission do you need to give yourself to take your own experience seriously?

4. *What is one structural factor in your current professional life that you know contributes to your exhaustion — and that you have not yet addressed? What has prevented you from addressing it?*

5. *If burnout is context-specific, do you still feel moments of genuine joy outside of work? Write about the last time you felt that. What does that memory tell you about what you still have access to?*

BEYOND STRESS:
THE HIDDEN COST OF BURNOUT

The full accounting — physical, cognitive, emotional, relational, professional

In the operating room, we use the term 'total body burden' to describe the cumulative physiological impact of surgery on a patient's system — the combined stress of anesthesia, blood loss, tissue trauma, fluid shifts, and the metabolic demands of healing. We monitor this carefully. We intervene when it exceeds safe limits. We do not simply add one more surgical insult because the patient is technically tolerating the current load. We understand that tolerance is not the same as health.

Burnout is the surgeon's total body burden. And like the post-operative patient, the surgeon who appears to be tolerating her load may be closer to a physiological crisis than anyone — including herself — realizes.

The Physical Cost: A Clinical Assessment

The relationship between chronic psychological stress and physical health outcomes is among the most well-documented in medicine. The mechanisms are well understood: sustained cortisol elevation disrupts virtually every major organ system. The immune system, cardiovascular system, gastrointestinal tract, endocrine system, and musculoskeletal system are all measurably affected by prolonged occupational stress.

★ Research Spotlight: Stress and Immune Function in Healthcare Workers

A landmark study published in Brain, Behavior, and Immunity found that healthcare workers under high occupational stress had significantly impaired natural killer cell activity and reduced vaccine response — meaning they were not only more susceptible to infection but less protected by the vaccinations they had received. A separate study in Psychosomatic Medicine found that chronically stressed physicians had measurably shorter telomeres — the chromosomal markers of cellular aging — compared to lower-stress controls, suggesting that occupational burnout may literally accelerate biological aging at the cellular level.

For the female surgeon specifically, the hormonal consequences of chronic stress deserve particular attention. The hypothalamic-pituitary-adrenal (HPA) axis, when chronically activated, suppresses the hypothalamic-pituitary-gonadal (HPG) axis — meaning that sustained occupational stress directly impacts reproductive hormone function. Menstrual irregularities, disrupted ovulation, and impacts on fertility have all been documented in women under sustained occupational stress. These are not hypothetical risks. They are documented clinical outcomes that the surgical culture has historically been too uncomfortable to discuss.

♦ Dr. Kezia | The Body's Ledger

Dr. Kezia had experienced three UTIs, two bouts of viral pharyngitis, a plantar fasciitis flare that had never fully resolved, and her first significant migraine episode — all within fourteen months. She attributed each one to a specific cause: poor fluid intake during long cases, a sick child at home, excessive standing, a stressful Q4. She was not wrong about the proximate causes. But she was missing the common thread: a chronically activated stress response that had left her immune system depleted, her inflammatory pathways upregulated, and her body running what she would have recognized in a patient as a negative energy balance. Her body had been keeping a ledger. She had not been reading it.

The Cognitive Cost: When the Scalpel-Sharp Mind Goes Dull

Surgical decision-making is one of the most cognitively demanding activities a human being can perform. It requires simultaneous integration of visual-spatial information, tactile feedback, anatomical memory, real-time problem-solving, team communication, and the management of uncertainty under time pressure — all while maintaining technical precision with instruments capable of causing serious harm. The margin for cognitive error in surgery is extremely small.

Burnout systematically erodes every one of these cognitive functions. Working memory capacity decreases under sustained stress — meaning the surgeon holds fewer pieces of information simultaneously with the same clarity she once had. Processing speed slows. Attentional flexibility — the ability to shift focus appropriately between the immediate task and the broader context — diminishes. And the inhibitory control that allows a surgeon to override an impulse when the anatomy surprises her weakens in proportion to prefrontal cortex dysfunction.

★ Research Spotlight: Cognitive Performance and Physician Fatigue

A study published in Annals of Surgery using neurocognitive testing found that surgeons performing after a night of disrupted sleep showed cognitive impairment equivalent to a blood alcohol level of 0.05%. A separate study found that burned-out physicians scored significantly lower on tests of executive function, working memory, and cognitive flexibility — the very capacities most essential to surgical decision-making. Importantly, the physicians themselves were poor judges of their own impairment. Like the impaired driver who feels fine to drive, the burned-out surgeon often feels she is performing normally when objective measures show otherwise.

◆ Dr. Sandra | The Chart She Almost Missed

Dr. Sandra was reviewing pre-op charts at 6:45 a.m. before a full day of pediatric cases. She had slept four hours, was on her second cup of coffee, and was carrying the background radiation of eighteen months of compounding burnout. She nearly signed off on a case without noting an allergy that had been added to the chart after her initial review. A medical student — rotating through her service, reading the chart for the first time — flagged it. Dr. Sandra thanked the student and returned to her office and sat very quietly for several minutes. She was not a careless surgeon. She was a burned-out one. In her mind, those had always been different things. In that moment, she understood they could converge.

The Emotional Cost: Compassion Fatigue and Moral Injury

Two distinct but related phenomena contribute to the emotional devastation of surgical burnout: compassion fatigue and moral injury. Understanding the difference between them is clinically important, because they respond to different interventions.

Compassion fatigue — also called secondary traumatic stress — is the emotional exhaustion that results from sustained empathic engagement with suffering. It is the cost of caring deeply, repeatedly, without sufficient recovery. The surgeon who has held the hands of frightened patients, delivered devastating diagnoses, and witnessed extreme suffering across thousands of patient encounters accumulates an emotional debt that, without adequate processing, becomes overwhelming. Compassion fatigue does not mean the surgeon has stopped caring. It means her capacity for care has been exhausted by overuse without replenishment.

Moral injury is a distinct phenomenon, first described in military veterans but increasingly recognized in healthcare workers. It occurs when a person is compelled to act in ways that violate their moral code — or is prevented from acting in ways that would uphold it — by forces beyond their control. For the surgeon, moral injury may arise from being compelled to discharge a patient before she is medically ready by insurance pressures. From watching a colleague behave unethically and feeling unable to intervene. From a system that prioritizes throughput over care. From witnessing a preventable complication that institutional inertia made inevitable. Moral injury is not burnout. But it accelerates and deepens burnout catastrophically.

◆ Dr. Michelle | Moral Injury and the System

Dr. Michelle spent three years fighting for the implementation of a screening protocol for a cancer disproportionately affecting underserved patients in her hospital's catchment area. She had the evidence. She had the data. She had the clinical rationale. She encountered institutional resistance at every level — budget constraints, competing priorities, the quiet inertia of a system that had not been designed with those patients in mind. When a thirty-eight-year-old woman presented with Stage IV disease that the protocol would almost certainly have caught at Stage I, Dr. Michelle sat with her patient's chart and felt something that was not grief, exactly, and not rage — though it contained elements of both. It was the specific desolation of moral injury: the knowledge that she had tried, that the system had failed, and that she would be expected to continue operating within that system as though the failure had not occurred.

The Relational Cost: What Burnout Does to the People You Love

The surgeon does not burn out in a vacuum. The burnout enters her home, her partnerships, her friendships, and her family. It alters the quality of her presence in every relationship she inhabits — not because she is a bad partner or parent or friend, but because the emotional and cognitive resources required for genuine connection are the same resources that burnout depletes.

Research on physician marriage and relationship satisfaction shows that burnout is among the strongest predictors of relational conflict and dissolution. The mechanisms are multiple: emotional withdrawal that partners experience as rejection; irritability that converts minor friction into major conflict; the physical absence of call schedules compounded by the psychological absence of burnout; and the gradual erosion of the shared life that sustained the relationship in the first place.

For the female surgeon with children, the relational cost carries an additional dimension. The cultural expectation that she will be simultaneously a fully present parent and a fully committed surgeon — without the institutional support that would make either possible — means she frequently fails at both by the standards she sets for herself. The guilt this generates is its own form of suffering, and it feeds directly back into the burnout cycle.

◆ Dr. Amara | The Dinner Table

Dr. Amara's son was eight years old when he began asking, at dinner, 'Mom, are you actually listening or are you just looking at me?' He asked it gently, without accusation — the way a child who loves his parent asks because he genuinely wants to know. She always said she was listening. And she was, technically — her eyes were on him, her phone was face down, she was attempting attention. But some part of her was still in the hospital. In the conversation with the family about the complication. In the chart she had not finished. In the committee report due Friday. Her son was not wrong. She was not fully there. The recognition of that — not once, but as a pattern — was one of the most painful and clarifying moments of her burnout journey. She had been losing him slowly, and he had noticed before she had.

✏ Reflection & Journaling Prompts

1. *Do an honest physical inventory. List every physical symptom you have experienced in the past six months that you have attributed to individual causes. What pattern do you see when you look at them together?*

2. *Describe a clinical error or near-miss you have experienced during a period of high stress. What does that experience tell you about the relationship between your cognitive performance and your wellbeing?*

3. *Is what you experience at work compassion fatigue, moral injury, or both? Write about a specific experience that fits each definition.*

4. *Write a letter from the perspective of someone who loves you, describing what they have observed in you over the past year. What would they say that you have not allowed yourself to hear?*

5. *What is the relational cost of your current burnout state? Be specific — name the relationships and describe the quality of your presence within them.*

Robert Amajoyi, MD; Ebere Jill Azumah, MD MPH

CHAPTER THREE
– EXPANDED

THE SCIENCE OF BURNOUT: BRAIN, BODY, AND EMOTIONS

A neurologist's map of what chronic stress does to the surgical mind

The surgeon who understands the neuroscience of burnout has a significant advantage over the one who simply knows it is happening. Understanding the mechanism — the specific biological processes by which chronic stress dismantles cognitive function, emotional regulation, and physical health — transforms burnout from a vague experiential malaise into a diagnosable condition with a rational treatment plan. This is the kind of thinking that surgeons are trained to do. It is time to apply it.

The Allostatic Load Concept

Allostasis refers to the body's ability to maintain stability through change — the active process of adaptation that allows us to respond to stressors and then return to baseline. Allostatic load refers to the cumulative cost of this repeated adaptation. Think of it as the wear and tear on the system that results from being mobilized repeatedly, without adequate recovery time between activations.

High allostatic load has been associated with accelerated cardiovascular aging, impaired immune function, metabolic disruption, cognitive decline, and significantly increased risk of mental health disorders. For the surgeon whose allostatic load has been elevated for years — through long hours, emotional labor, physical demands, sleep disruption, and the specific stressors of navigating a high-stakes professional environment — this is not abstract. It is measurable, and it is consequential.

★ Research Spotlight: Allostatic Load in Surgical Residents

A study published in the Journal of Surgical Education found measurably elevated allostatic load markers — including elevated cortisol, disrupted heart rate variability, and altered inflammatory cytokine profiles — in surgical residents compared to age-matched controls in non-medical professions. These markers were detectable within the first year of residency and worsened progressively across training years. The study also found that residents who reported higher levels of social support and regular recovery activities showed significantly lower allostatic load scores, providing direct evidence that the interventions described in this book have measurable biological impact.

The Prefrontal Cortex Under Fire

The prefrontal cortex (PFC) is the part of the brain most relevant to what we think of as surgical excellence: deliberate decision-making, impulse control, working memory, emotional regulation, and the ability to hold multiple competing priorities in mind simultaneously while acting precisely. It is the executive center of the surgical brain. And it is the part of the brain most vulnerable to disruption by chronic stress.

The mechanism is well-characterized. Under acute stress, norepinephrine and dopamine are released in the PFC in carefully calibrated amounts that actually enhance performance — this is the neurochemical basis of the surgical 'flow state' that experienced surgeons recognize. But under chronic stress, these neurotransmitters are released in excessive and dysregulated amounts, triggering a shift in PFC function that progressively impairs its capacity for executive control. The PFC becomes less efficient, slower, and more likely to be overridden by more primitive brain structures — particularly the amygdala.

This has a specific surgical implication: the surgeon experiencing chronic burnout is less able to override a first impulse when the anatomy surprises her, less able to make the subtle judgment calls that distinguish good surgical outcomes from great ones, and less able to regulate her emotional responses to the inevitable frustrations of a complex case. The hands may still perform. The judgment is quietly compromised.

The Amygdala's Alarm and the Threat-Saturated Surgeon

The amygdala is the brain's threat-detection system — a rapid, subcortical processor that evaluates incoming information for potential danger and, when it detects a threat, triggers the stress response before the conscious mind has even registered what is happening. In a healthy, rested brain, the PFC modulates the amygdala's reactivity — providing contextual information that allows appropriate assessment of whether a perceived threat is actually dangerous.

In the burned-out brain, this modulation is impaired. The amygdala becomes hyperreactive — detecting threat in situations that a rested mind would assess as manageable. The resident's question feels like a challenge. The administrator's email feels like an attack. The unexpected finding in the OR feels catastrophic rather than merely challenging. The surgeon is not overreacting out of character. Her threat-detection system has been recalibrated by chronic stress — and it is now detecting threats at a lower threshold, with a more intense response, and with less effective modulation than it should.

♦ Dr. Priya | The Amygdala in the Conference Room

During a morbidity and mortality conference, Dr. Priya presented a case involving a post-operative complication she had managed appropriately. A senior surgeon asked a question about her intraoperative decision-making — a standard M&M question, asked in the collegial tone these conferences typically employ. Dr. Priya felt her heart rate climb immediately. Her hands went cold. She experienced what she could only describe as a flash of terror that was completely disproportionate to the situation. She answered the question. She answered it well. But the physiological activation took forty minutes to fully resolve. Her amygdala, primed by months of accumulated stress, had processed a routine question as an existential threat. She recognized this later, when she had language for it. In the moment, she thought it meant she was falling apart.

Neuroplasticity: The Brain's Capacity for Recovery

Here is the other side of the neuroscience — and it is important. The same neuroplasticity that allows chronic stress to dismantle prefrontal function and sensitize the amygdala also allows recovery to rebuild them. The brain is not static. It responds to experience — and deliberate recovery experiences can measurably restore the neural architecture that burnout has damaged.

Consistent sleep improves prefrontal metabolic function. Regular aerobic exercise promotes hippocampal neurogenesis —literally growing new neurons in the structure most vulnerable to stress-related shrinkage. Mindfulness practice has been shown in multiple neuroimaging studies to reduce amygdala reactivity and strengthen the PFC-amygdala regulatory pathway. Social connection activates the brain's reward and safety circuits, providing neurochemical counterbalance to the threat activation of chronic stress. These are not soft wellness concepts. They are evidence-based neural interventions.

★ Research Spotlight: Mindfulness and Brain Structure in Physicians

A study published in NeuroImage found that physicians who completed an eight-week mindfulness-based stress reduction (MBSR) program showed measurable increases in gray matter density in the PFC and hippocampus, and measurable decreases in amygdala gray matter density — changes in the direction opposite to those produced by chronic stress. Importantly, these structural changes were detectable after just eight weeks of practice averaging twenty-seven minutes per day. The brain does not require years of meditation retreat. It requires consistent, deliberate recovery practice — at a scale that is actually achievable in a surgical life.

◆ Dr. Kezia | The Recovery Experiment

Dr. Kezia was skeptical of mindfulness. She was also, after eighteen months of progressive burnout, desperate enough to try anything. She downloaded a guided meditation application and committed to ten minutes each morning before leaving for the hospital — not because she believed it would work, but because it was ten minutes and she had nothing to lose. At six weeks, she noticed she was sleeping more deeply. At ten weeks, a colleague commented that she seemed less reactive in difficult situations. At fourteen weeks, she reviewed her allostatic load — not with a formal study, but with a personal inventory — and found that the physical symptoms she had been cataloguing had begun, slowly, to improve. The practice was not magic. It was neuroscience. The brain had begun, given the opportunity, to heal itself.

✏ Reflection & Journaling Prompts

1. *Think of a recent situation in which your response seemed disproportionate to the actual threat. Looking back through the lens of amygdala hyperreactivity, what do you understand now that you did not understand then?*

2. *What does your working memory feel like right now compared to five years ago? Where do you notice the cognitive cost of burnout most clearly in your daily work?*

3. *Which of the neuroplasticity interventions described — sleep, exercise, mindfulness, social connection — is most absent from your current life? What is the real barrier to incorporating it?*

4. *If you could give your brain one restorative gift this week that costs nothing but time, what would it be? What would it take to protect that time?*

5. *Write a clinical case note about yourself as a patient presenting with the symptoms of burnout. What would you prescribe? What follow-up plan would you recommend?*

Robert Amajoyi, MD; Ebere Jill Azumah, MD MPH

CHAPTER FOUR
– EXPANDED

WHY BURNOUT IS MORE COMMON THAN YOU THINK

*The structural, cultural, and societal forces
producing a professional epidemic*

Burnout among surgeons did not happen because surgeons became weaker. It happened because the demands placed on surgeons became greater while the resources provided to support them remained, at best, static. This distinction matters enormously — because the narrative of individual weakness locates the solution inside the individual, while the narrative of systemic failure demands both individual and systemic response. Both are necessary. But without understanding the systemic dimension, the individual is left fighting a structural problem with personal tools — and wondering why the tools are not enough.

Robert Amajoyi, MD; Ebere Jill Azumah, MD MPH

The Structural Drivers of Surgical Burnout

The structural contributors to burnout in surgery are well-documented and largely unaddressed. They include: unsustainable call schedules that have not meaningfully changed despite mounting evidence of their cognitive and safety consequences; administrative burden that has grown exponentially with the introduction of electronic health records, consuming time previously available for patient care and recovery; production pressure that ties institutional revenue to surgical volume in ways that create implicit incentives for overwork; inadequate staffing that means nurses, residents, and support staff are also burned out, compounding the burden on the attending surgeon; and the fundamental mismatch between the 24/7 demands of surgical illness and the finite capacity of the human beings who respond to them.

★ Research Spotlight: Administrative Burden and Physician Burnout

A 2022 report from the National Academy of Medicine found that physicians spend an average of 4.5 hours per day on administrative tasks in the electronic health record — time that is not reimbursed, not recognized in most workload calculations, and not offset by any reduction in clinical expectations. This 'pajama time' — named for the evening hours physicians spend completing documentation after their families have gone to bed — was identified as one of the single strongest predictors of burnout across all specialties. Surgical specialties, with their high case volume and complex operative documentation requirements, reported some of the highest administrative burden scores.

The Gender-Specific Burden

The burnout literature is unequivocal on this point: female physicians experience burnout at higher rates than their male counterparts, and the contributing factors are not simply more work — they are different work, layered on top of the same work, in a culture that frequently does not acknowledge either the difference or the additional weight.

The gender-specific contributors to burnout in surgery include: implicit and explicit bias in evaluation, promotion, and recognition; the higher rates of sexual harassment and workplace discrimination that female surgeons report; the disproportionate allocation of 'office housework' — committee service, mentoring, administrative tasks that advance institutional goals without advancing individual careers; the work-home conflict that falls more heavily on women in dual-career households; the penalty, real or perceived, for utilizing parental leave and the career consequences that follow it; and the emotional labor of being among the first or few in a specialty or institution — of representing not just oneself but every woman who comes after, in every room, every day.

This burden is real. It is documented. It is not a complaint — it is a clinical finding. And its inclusion in any honest discussion of burnout among female surgeons is not optional. To address burnout in this population without naming these structural contributors is to treat the symptom while leaving the pathology in place.

♦ Dr. Michelle | The Invisible Tax

In a single academic year, Dr. Michelle served on four departmental committees, mentored eleven residents and medical students, delivered three grand rounds presentations at other institutions, chaired a diversity task force that met monthly and produced a fifty-page report, and maintained her full clinical and operative schedule. When she submitted her portfolio for promotion review, the committee noted that her research output was 'below expectations for this career stage.' Not one of the items on her committee and mentoring list counted toward the productivity metrics on which she was evaluated. She had spent an entire year doing work that the institution valued — evidenced by the fact that they had asked her to do it — and that the institution's promotion system did not recognize. She did not make a scene. She went back to her office and began a research project she had not had time to start. And she carried the weight of the year's invisible labor forward into the next year, where it was waiting to be added to the next year's load.

The Culture of Silence

One of the most powerful perpetuators of surgical burnout is the culture of silence around its experience. The surgeon who would immediately refer a patient showing signs of a serious illness to a specialist will often spend years minimizing, rationalizing, and concealing her own symptoms from colleagues, supervisors, and herself.

This silence is not weakness. It is rational. In a culture where mental health struggles are associated — explicitly or implicitly — with questions about clinical competence and licensure, where professional identity is built on the perception of invulnerability, and where disclosing difficulty may result in reduced opportunity or increased scrutiny, the decision to remain silent about burnout is entirely understandable. It is also, cumulatively, killing people.

★ Research Spotlight: Stigma and Help-Seeking in Surgeons

A survey of more than 7,000 surgeons published in JAMA Surgery found that while 60% of respondents met criteria for burnout on validated screening tools, fewer than 15% had sought any form of professional mental health support in the preceding year. The most commonly cited barriers were stigma (named by 68% of respondents), concerns about confidentiality (58%), concerns about impact on licensure (52%), and lack of time (71%). Notably, female surgeons were somewhat more likely than male counterparts to have sought support — but also more likely to report that disclosure had negatively affected how they were perceived by peers.

◆ Dr. Sandra | Breaking the Silence

Dr. Sandra finally told her department chief that she was struggling. Not because she was ready to — she was not. She told him because a senior colleague who had noticed her decline mentioned it to her first, in private, with care: 'Sandra, I am not your chief right now. I am your colleague. What is happening?' She cried in her office for the first time in eleven years. She then made an appointment with the employee assistance program. And she began, slowly and carefully, to rebuild. The chief's response was not punitive. It was supportive. She had been afraid of a conversation that turned out to be one of the most important professional experiences of her career. She had let the fear of the imagined response delay the actual response by more than a year.

➡ Reflection & Journaling Prompts

1. *Which of the structural contributors to burnout described in this chapter are present in your current professional environment? Which ones have you accepted as simply 'how things are'?*

2. *What is the gender-specific burden you carry that has not been fully acknowledged by your institution or your colleagues? Write it out in detail.*

3. *What has kept you silent about your burnout? Name the specific fear. Then ask: what is the actual probability that this fear would materialize if you spoke honestly?*

4. *Is there one colleague whose burnout you have noticed but not named? What would it mean to approach them the way Dr. Sandra's colleague approached her?*

5. *If the culture of silence in surgery is a systemic problem, what is one thing you could do — as an attending, a chief, a mentor, or a peer — to begin dismantling it in your specific environment?*

13 SIGNS OF BURNOUT
— AND SPOTTING THEM EARLY

*The diagnostic skill set turned inward — reading
your own signals with clinical honesty*

The surgeon is, by training, a diagnostician. She has spent years developing the capacity to observe, interpret, and act on clinical signals — to read a patient's presentation with precision and arrive at a diagnosis that may not be immediately obvious. This same capacity, directed inward, is the most important early warning system she possesses for burnout. The challenge is that the skills of inward observation are not taught in surgical training, and the culture actively discourages their use.

What follows is an expansion of the thirteen signs previously introduced, with greater clinical depth, surgeon-specific manifestation, and specific self-assessment guidance. Read these not as items on a checklist but as clinical findings requiring the same honest, dispassionate assessment you would apply to a complex patient presentation.

The Early Signs: Stage One

The following signs typically appear in the exhaustion stage of burnout — the earliest and most treatable phase. If you recognize yourself primarily in these descriptions, you have a significant opportunity to intervene before the cycle deepens.

1. Fatigue that sleep does not resolve

This is qualitatively different from post-call tiredness, which improves predictably with recovery sleep. Burnout fatigue is deeper — a bone-level weariness that eight or nine hours of sleep leaves essentially unchanged. It is the fatigue of a depleted system, not a tired one. If you have slept well and still feel fundamentally exhausted, the problem is not sleep debt. It is systemic depletion. Self-assessment: Rate your energy level on a Monday morning after a non-call weekend on a scale of 1-10. If it is consistently below 6, this sign is present.

2. Increased physical symptoms without clear cause

Headaches that appear mid-morning and resolve incompletely. Gastrointestinal upset that your gastroenterologist cannot find a structural explanation for. Muscle tension in the neck and upper back that massage therapy improves but does not resolve. Frequent minor infections. These are the body's burnout language. Self-assessment: List your physical complaints of the past six months. How many have you investigated and found structurally normal? What other explanation have you considered?

3. Declining interest in continuing education

The surgeon who once read journals with genuine curiosity, who attended conferences to learn rather than to maintain CME credits, who sought out new techniques with enthusiasm — if she finds that professional reading has become an obligation she avoids rather than a pleasure she pursues, this is an early warning sign. The intellectual appetite that drives surgical excellence requires adequate fuel. Burnout depletes it.

The Middle Signs: Stage Two

These signs indicate that burnout has progressed beyond exhaustion into detachment. Intervention at this stage requires more significant structural change and more deliberate recovery work.

4. Emotional numbness with patients

The surgeon who once felt a particular kind of satisfaction when explaining a diagnosis clearly and watching a patient's anxiety reduce — if she finds that patient interactions have become functional rather than meaningful, that she is going through the motions of compassion rather than actually experiencing it, this is a significant warning sign. It is also frequently invisible to patients, which can make it easier to ignore. Self-assessment: In your last week of patient interactions, can you name a specific moment that felt genuinely connecting? If not — when was the last one you can remember?

5. Cynicism and negativity about the profession

Every surgeon has moments of frustration with the healthcare system, institutional bureaucracy, and the limitations of medicine. But a pervasive, generalized cynicism — a sense that the system is irreparably broken, that the work is ultimately futile, that patients are ungrateful or the institution is irredeemably corrupt — is different in quality from normal professional frustration. It is the emotional detachment of burnout expressing itself as philosophy.

6. Interpersonal friction with colleagues and staff

The burned-out surgeon is more likely to have conflicts with nursing staff, residents, and administrative personnel — not because she has become a different person, but because the amygdala hyperreactivity described in the previous chapter means that ordinary friction now triggers a stress response that previously would not have registered. If you are receiving more feedback about your interpersonal style, or noticing more conflict in relationships that were previously smooth — this is clinical information.

♦ Dr. Amara | The Staff Feedback

The OR charge nurse stopped by Dr. Amara's office after a particularly difficult case — not to report a problem, but because she had worked with Dr. Amara for six years and recognized something was wrong. 'Dr. Amara,' she said, 'you have always been direct with the team. But lately it's felt different. It feels like you're angry at us. We're not sure what we're doing wrong.' Dr. Amara had not been aware of the change. She thought of herself as direct and appropriately demanding. Her team — who had been with her for years and knew her baseline — were perceiving something different. She took the feedback seriously. It told her something her own introspection had been unable to surface.

The Advanced Signs: Stage Three

These signs indicate that burnout has progressed to a stage where professional performance is being meaningfully affected. If you recognize yourself primarily in these descriptions, the urgency for intervention is high — and professional support, including therapy and potentially medical evaluation, is appropriate.

7. Thoughts of leaving surgery

Passing thoughts of career change are normal across any professional life. But persistent, serious contemplation of leaving surgery — particularly among surgeons who have given no indication of wanting to do so previously — is a significant warning sign. This is not necessarily evidence that surgery is wrong for this person. It is often evidence that burnout has made surgery feel impossible in its current form. These thoughts deserve evaluation, not dismissal.

8. Detachment from outcomes

The surgeon who has lost the emotional investment in her outcomes — who feels neither satisfaction at a successful case nor appropriate concern at a complication — has reached a stage of detachment that represents a significant patient safety concern as well as a personal crisis. This is not the equanimity of the experienced clinician who processes outcomes with appropriate perspective. It is the flatness of a depleted system.

9. Suicidal ideation

Physicians, including surgeons, experience suicidal ideation at rates significantly higher than the general population. If you are experiencing thoughts of suicide or self-harm, this requires immediate professional intervention. The National Suicide Prevention Lifeline is available at 988. The Physician Support Line (1-888-409-0141) offers free, confidential peer support specifically for physicians. These resources exist because you are not alone in this, and because help is available.

✓ Practical Action: Early Burnout Screening — A Self-Assessment Protocol

- Rate your energy level on Monday morning after a non-call weekend (1-10). Consistent score below 6 = Stage 1 concern.

- Count the number of patient interactions in the past week that felt genuinely connecting. If you cannot name one, note the date.

- List your physical complaints over the past 6 months. Circle those with no identified structural cause.

- Ask a trusted colleague or family member: 'Have you noticed any changes in me in the past year?' Listen without defending.

- Complete the Maslach Burnout Inventory (MBI) — available online — as an objective baseline measure.

☞ Reflection & Journaling Prompts

1. *Which of the 13 signs do you recognize most clearly in yourself right now? Which have you been most actively minimizing or rationalizing?*

2. *At what stage of burnout do you assess yourself to be — exhaustion, detachment, or loss of effectiveness? What would it change about your approach if you accepted that assessment?*

3. *Think of a colleague you believe is experiencing burnout. What signs are you observing? Now turn the same observation toward yourself.*

4. *What is the earliest sign that appears in your experience when burnout is beginning to cycle? If you could notice that sign earlier and respond to it immediately, what would your response be?*

5. *Write a personal 'burnout early warning protocol' — the three signs that, if present, indicate you need to take immediate recovery action, and the three specific actions you will take.*

Robert Amajoyi, MD; Ebere Jill Azumah, MD MPH

CHAPTER SIX
– EXPANDED

WHY WE BURN OUT IN OUR MODERN LIVES

*The perfect storm of structure,
culture, identity, and demand*

Burnout does not happen because the surgeon is not strong enough. It happens because she is operating inside a system that was not designed for sustainable human performance — a system that mistakes endurance for excellence, that conflates quantity of hours with quality of care, and that has historically rewarded the behaviors most likely to produce burnout while stigmatizing the practices most likely to prevent it. Understanding the specific forces that produce burnout in the surgical life is not an exercise in excuse-making. It is the precondition for designing a rational and effective response.

The Perfectionism Trap in Surgery

Perfectionism is not a personality quirk in surgery — it is a survival mechanism that the training system deliberately cultivates. The resident who is expected to have read every article, to know every anatomical variant, to have anticipated every complication before it occurred — she is being trained to hold herself to a standard that is, by definition, impossible to achieve. And she is being trained to feel responsible, and ashamed, when she falls short of it.

The clinical costs of this cultivated perfectionism are well-documented. Perfectionism predicts burnout through multiple pathways: it prevents the surgeon from delegating effectively, compresses her capacity to tolerate the normal uncertainty of clinical practice, converts every complication into a referendum on her worth as a surgeon and a person, and makes recovery — which inherently involves accepting imperfection — psychologically threatening rather than restorative.

★ Research Spotlight: Perfectionism, Self-Compassion, and Surgeon Wellbeing

Research published in the British Journal of Surgery found that surgeons who scored high on measures of maladaptive perfectionism and low on self-compassion had burnout rates more than twice those of surgeons with the inverse profile — despite working similar hours and managing similar caseloads. The study's conclusion was striking: the internal relationship the surgeon had with her own performance was a stronger predictor of burnout than the external demands of the job. This finding points directly toward the intervention that most surgeons find most counterintuitive: treating themselves with the same standard of care they would apply to a patient.

♦ Dr. Priya | The Perfect Standard

Dr. Priya's program director told her, during her mid-year review, that she was performing in the top quartile of her fellowship cohort. She went home and spent two hours reviewing the cases in which she felt she had not met her own standard. There were seven. She catalogued each one. She reviewed the literature on each operative decision she had made differently than she would have made in retrospect. By the end of the evening, she had confirmed, with evidence, that in five of the seven cases she had performed correctly. In two, she had made reasonable decisions that, with the benefit of hindsight and better information, she might have made differently. None of these distinctions produced relief. She still felt that she had failed. Her perfectionism had made her impervious to evidence of her own excellence.

The Work-Home Interface: A System Under Impossible Pressure

The dual demands of surgical career and personal life do not exist in separate compartments that the surgeon can attend to in sequence. They are simultaneous, overlapping, and frequently in direct conflict — and the infrastructure available to navigate that conflict has not kept pace with the increasing participation of women in surgery.

Consider the arithmetic: A female surgeon who is also a primary parent manages school pickups that cannot be rescheduled, pediatrician appointments that cannot be delegated, the invisible logistics of a household that require cognitive presence even when physical presence is impossible, and the emotional labor of maintaining relationships that sustain her family's wellbeing — all while maintaining a surgical practice that demands physical presence, cognitive intensity, and temporal unpredictability that is incompatible with the fixed schedules of family life. The system has not solved this problem. It has largely asked the woman to solve it herself.

◆ Dr. Sandra | The Impossible Schedule

On a Tuesday in February, Dr. Sandra had a complex pediatric case that ran ninety minutes over schedule, a post-operative complication that required her immediate presence in the PICU, a grant deadline she had been working toward for six months, a parent-teacher conference at her son's school that she had promised she would attend, and a babysitter who called at 4:15 p.m. to say she was ill. She managed the complication. She missed the conference. She called the babysitter's backup. She asked her husband — who had his own demanding schedule — to leave work early. She submitted a draft of the grant at 11:47 p.m. that she knew was not as strong as it could have been. None of this was unusual. It was, in fact, a fairly ordinary Tuesday. She lay awake afterward not thinking about the complication — she had managed it well and the child was stable — but thinking about her son's face when she had texted that she would not be there. The case had not broken her. The conference had.

Racism, Bias, and the Compound Burden

Any honest discussion of burnout in female surgery must name what the data consistently confirm: surgeons from racial and ethnic minority groups experience burnout at higher rates, and the contributing factors include not only the structural drivers shared by all surgeons but the additional, compounding weight of racial bias, cultural isolation, tokenism, and the emotional labor of navigating environments that have not been designed with their presence in mind.

The surgeon who is both a woman and a person of color navigates a double minority status in a profession whose demographics have historically been overwhelmingly white and male. She may be the first in her department. She may be the only one in her operative suite. She may be expected to serve simultaneously as a clinical surgeon, a diversity ambassador, a mentor to all underrepresented students who rotate through her service, and a spokesperson for institutional diversity initiatives — while also maintaining the research productivity, clinical volume, and administrative contributions expected of any surgeon at her level. The compound burden is real. The burnout it produces is predictable. And the silence around it — in the interest of appearing strong, not confirming stereotypes, not providing ammunition to those who question her fitness — is its own form of suffering.

♦ Dr. Michelle | The Weight of Being First

Dr. Michelle was the first Black female attending in her department's history. She had been celebrated for this distinction at her hiring. Three years in, she understood what the celebration had not prepared her for: the particular exhaustion of being perpetually visible, perpetually representative, and perpetually evaluated through a lens that her white male colleagues were not. Every error she made was potentially evidence of a pattern. Every success she achieved was potentially attributed to affirmative action. Every difficulty she raised was potentially confirmation of a bias that suggested she didn't belong. She navigated all of this in addition to a full surgical caseload, a research portfolio, a teaching role, and a family that needed more of her than she had left to give. She did not call it burnout for a long time. She called it the cost of being here. Eventually she learned that the cost did not have to be this high.

➥ Reflection & Journaling Prompts

1. *Describe your relationship with perfectionism. In what specific situations does it serve you? In what situations does it harm you? What would 'good enough' look like in those situations?*

2. *Map the work-home interface of your current life. What is in conflict, what is in competition, and what institutional support is absent that would make the conflict manageable?*

3. *What compound burdens do you carry that most of your*

colleagues do not? Have you ever fully named them — to yourself, to a mentor, to your institution?

4. *Which of the burnout causes described in this chapter — work-related, personal/lifestyle, psychological, environmental — is most dominant in your experience? What would addressing it actually require?*

5. *Write a letter to your program director, chief, or institution describing what they could change that would most significantly reduce your burnout risk. You do not have to send it. But write it.*

Robert Amajoyi, MD; Ebere Jill Azumah, MD MPH

CHAPTER SEVEN
– EXPANDED

BREAKING FREE FROM THE CYCLE

The architecture of escape — and why the cycle is harder to break than it appears

The burnout cycle is self-perpetuating by design — not through malice, but through the very mechanisms that make it feel impossible to escape. The exhausted person does not have the energy to make the changes that would reduce her exhaustion. The detached person cannot access the motivation that would drive her to seek recovery. The person who has lost effectiveness may not have the clarity to identify what effectiveness would even look like. Understanding this self-referential trap is the first step toward dismantling it.

Why the 'Just Rest' Solution Fails

The most common advice given to burned-out surgeons is to rest — to take a vacation, to take time off, to slow down. This advice is not wrong. Rest is necessary. But it is insufficient alone — and when offered without attention to the structural conditions that produced the burnout, it is essentially a recommendation to refuel and then return to a vehicle with a broken engine. The fuel will be consumed at the same rate. The breakdown will come again, sooner and harder.

The research on physician burnout interventions is instructive here: individual-level interventions — vacation, mindfulness training, stress management workshops — show modest, short-term effects on burnout scores. Structural interventions — reduced administrative burden, protected time, schedule control, adequate staffing — show more sustained effects. The most effective approach combines both: addressing the individual's capacity for recovery while simultaneously addressing the structural conditions that deplete that capacity faster than it can be restored.

The Five Leverage Points for Cycle Interruption

Rather than attempting to change everything at once — which is itself a perfectionist trap that burnout makes cognitively impossible — the most effective approach to cycle interruption focuses on five high-leverage points where relatively small changes produce disproportionate impact.

Leverage Point 1: The First Recovery Window

Within the burnout cycle, there is typically a brief period following crisis or collapse where the person has genuine energy for change. This is the moment when a serious illness forces two weeks of rest, or an ultimatum from a partner demands a real renegotiation, or a department chief has a direct conversation about performance. This window is narrow and precious. The surgeon who uses it only to recover and return to baseline — rather than to make structural changes that alter the conditions causing the burnout — will enter the next rotation of the cycle with higher baseline depletion than the previous one.

Leverage Point 2: The Overcommitment Decision

The burnout cycle begins with overcommitment — the moment when the surgeon accepts more than she can sustainably manage. This decision is made in discrete, identifiable moments: the additional committee, the extra case block, the yes to the thing she should have declined. Developing a decision-making protocol for these moments — a pause, a review of current capacity, a question ('what would I need to remove to add this?') — interrupts the cycle before it begins.

Leverage Point 3: The Self-Care Non-Negotiables

The cycle accelerates when self-care activities are the first to be sacrificed to workload pressure. This is functionally backwards — because self-care is what maintains the capacity to sustain workload. Identifying two or three specific self-care practices as genuine non-negotiables — protected with the same force as OR block time — removes them from the sacrifice pool and slows the cycle's acceleration.

Leverage Point 4: The Early Warning Signal

Every surgeon has an idiosyncratic early warning signal for burnout — a specific symptom or behavior that appears reliably in the earliest stages of the cycle, before significant damage is done. For one surgeon it is the quality of her sleep. For another it is the irritability she shows in morning rounds. For a third it is the avoidance of a particular type of administrative task. Identifying this signal and responding to it as a clinical finding — rather than pushing through it — converts a reactive intervention into a proactive one.

Leverage Point 5: The Accountability Relationship

The burnout cycle is much harder to sustain in the presence of an honest accountability relationship — a mentor, peer, therapist, or partner who has been given explicit permission to name what they observe. This relationship does not guarantee cycle interruption. But it provides an external perspective that the burned-out person's impaired self-assessment cannot provide, and that has been shown in multiple studies to be among the strongest protective factors against burnout relapse.

♦ Dr. Amara | The Cycle Map

Over a three-day period during a conference trip — the first time she had been alone and unscheduled in more than a year — Dr. Amara drew her burnout cycle on a piece of hotel stationery. She mapped: the trigger events (the committee request, the chair's ask, the resident who needed extra supervision), the compensatory behaviors (giving up the morning run, stopping meal prep, staying later), the acceleration phase (the headaches, the sleep disruption, the irritability), the crisis point (the tearful conversation with her husband that had produced a week of temporary relief), and the return to baseline conditions. She looked at the map for a long time. 'I keep solving the same problem wrong,' she said to herself. Then she identified her five leverage points and spent the rest of the conference developing a specific plan for each one.

✓ Practical Action: Your Personal Cycle Interruption Protocol

- Draw your burnout cycle: trigger → stress build → exhaustion → detachment → crisis → recovery → return

- Identify your personal early warning signal — the first symptom that reliably appears in Stage 1

- List three current overcommitments you could exit or renegotiate within the next 30 days

- Name two self-care practices that are currently negotiable that you will make non-negotiable

- Identify one person who will serve as your accountability relationship for the next 90 days

✒ Reflection & Journaling Prompts

1. *Map your personal burnout cycle from the last time you clearly experienced it. Where exactly did it begin? Where were the moments when intervention was possible but did not occur?*

2. *What is your personal early warning signal for burnout onset? How quickly do you typically recognize it? How do you typically respond to it?*

3. *Of the five leverage points described in this chapter, which one would have the greatest impact on your cycle if you addressed it? What specifically would addressing it require?*

4. *Think about the last time you had genuine recovery energy — the moment after a crisis when you felt capable of change. Did you use that window for structural change or for returning to baseline? What would you do differently now?*

5. *Who is your accountability relationship? If that person does not currently exist, who in your life has the trust, insight, and honesty to serve in that role? What would it take to ask them?*

CHAPTER EIGHT – EXPANDED

THE MINDSET SHIFT: PERMISSION TO REST

Rewriting the story the surgical culture wrote inside you

The surgeon who needs permission to rest has already identified something important: that the prohibition against rest is not coming from her clinical schedule, her patients, or her institution. It is coming from inside her — from a story about what rest means that was written during her training and has been reinforcing itself ever since. Changing that story is not a matter of willpower. It is a matter of understanding where the story came from, recognizing it as a story rather than a fact, and deliberately replacing it with something truer.

Where the Story Came From

The story that rest is weakness did not arrive fully formed. It was assembled from hundreds of small messages received across years of surgical training: the attending who arrived before anyone else and left last; the residency culture that celebrated the person who seemed to need the least sleep; the implicit evaluation of commitment measured by hours in the building; the senior surgeon who mentioned, in passing, that she had not taken a vacation in four years, as though this were a mark of distinction rather than a symptom. These messages accumulated. They became belief. And belief, unchallenged, becomes identity.

The identity component is crucial. The surgeon who believes that rest is weakness does not merely avoid rest out of busyness — she avoids it out of self-concept. To rest is to become someone she does not recognize: a surgeon who is not, at every moment, maximally productive and available. This is why the behavioral change of 'just take a break' is insufficient without the cognitive change of 'rest is not a threat to who I am.' The behavior and the belief must change together.

★ Research Spotlight: Identity Threat and Physician Recovery

Research in occupational psychology has documented that professionals with highly fused professional identities — those for whom the work role is central to self-concept — recover more slowly from occupational stress than those with broader, more differentiated identities. For physicians, who undergo one of the most identity-transforming educational experiences in professional life, this fusion is nearly universal. The practical implication is clear: building a sense of self that is not entirely dependent on surgical performance is not a philosophical luxury. It is a burnout prevention strategy with measurable impact.

The Permission Statement Practice

Permission statements are not affirmations — they are cognitive reframes designed to address the specific belief patterns that make rest feel like transgression. Unlike affirmations, which assert a positive without addressing the underlying negative, permission statements directly name the prohibition and replace it with an evidence-based alternative.

'Resting is how I maintain the quality of care my patients deserve.'

This reframe is clinically accurate. The rested surgeon is the safer surgeon. The recovered surgeon makes better decisions. Rest is not separate from patient care — it is a component of it. When the prohibition against rest says 'rest is selfish,' this reframe says 'rest is professional responsibility.'

'My value as a surgeon is not measured by how much I sacrifice.'

This reframe addresses the productivity-as-worth equation directly. The surgeon who performs eight well-considered cases delivers more value than the same surgeon performing twelve exhausted ones. Quality of presence is a measure of surgical value. Quantity of hours is a measure of endurance.

'I am a person first and a surgeon second — and neither is sustainable without the other.'

This reframe addresses the identity fusion that makes rest feel threatening. The person exists independently of the surgeon. The person has needs that are not subordinate to the surgical career. Both are true simultaneously, and honoring the person does not diminish the surgeon.

'What I do during rest is preparation — not absence.'

High-performance athletes in every discipline build structured recovery into their training protocols because they understand that adaptation — strength, skill, endurance — happens during recovery, not during performance. The surgeon who rests is not away from her work. She is doing the work of recovery.

◆ Dr. Kezia | The Permission Process

Dr. Kezia kept a small card in her white coat pocket on which she had written three permission statements — the three that most directly addressed the specific prohibitions that had been most damaging in her case. Whenever she felt the pull to extend her day unnecessarily, to skip a meal, or to respond to a non-urgent message at 10 p.m., she read the card. Not as a ritual, but as a clinical reminder — a prescription she had written for herself and that she was required, as a professional, to follow. 'If I wrote this for a patient,' she had told herself when she made the card, 'I would expect compliance. The same standard applies to me.'

Redefining Productivity for the Sustainable Surgeon

The surgical culture defines productivity in terms of output: cases per week, patients seen per day, publications per year, committees served. This is a legitimate metric for some purposes. But as the primary measure of a surgeon's worth, it is incomplete — because it measures production without accounting for the cost of that production or its sustainability over time.

A broader definition of surgical productivity would include: the quality and safety of outcomes over time; the development of trainees; the strength of patient relationships; the capacity to sustain excellent practice across a full career; and the maintenance of the person behind the surgeon in a state that permits genuine engagement with her work. By this broader definition, rest and recovery are not interruptions to productivity. They are components of it.

The surgeon who works at 70% of her sustainable capacity for thirty years will produce more — safer, better, more thoughtfully — than the surgeon who works at 110% of her sustainable capacity for fifteen years, burns out, and exits the profession or remains within it in a state of chronic compromise. The mathematics of sustainable practice favor the surgeon who rests.

Reflection & Journaling Prompts

1. *Write down the most powerful story you tell yourself about why you cannot rest. Where did this story come from? Is it true — or is it the training culture speaking through you?*

2. *Which of the permission statements in this chapter most directly addresses a belief that limits you? Rewrite it in your own words, specific to your situation.*

3. *By the broader definition of productivity described in this chapter, how do you assess your own productivity? What would change about your daily schedule if you embraced this definition?*

4. *Describe the last time you truly rested — not slept, but genuinely restored yourself. What did that feel like? What made it possible? What would it take to create that experience more regularly?*

5. *What is one rest practice you could schedule this week as a non-negotiable — and what specifically would you need to decline or defer in order to protect it?*

STRESS MANAGEMENT TOOLS FOR DAILY LIFE

*Practical tools built for the actual
margins of the surgical schedule*

The Non-Negotiation of Micro-Recovery

One of the most persistent myths in surgical culture is that meaningful stress management requires signifi-cant time — a full vacation, a weekend retreat, an extended leave. The research does not support this. What it consistently shows is that frequent, brief recovery interventions — distributed throughout the day rather than accumulated at its end — are more effective at regulating cortisol levels and maintaining cognitive function than infrequent, extended ones. The surgeon who takes five two-minute breathing resets across a twelve-hour day manages her neurochemical load more effectively than the one who powers through and collapses at home. Micro-recovery is not a concession to weakness. It is evidence-based performance management.

The Body Is the First Responder

The body-based stress management strategies described in this book — deep breathing, progressive muscle relaxation, movement, grounding — work because they act directly on the autonomic nervous system, shifting it from sympathetic dominance (fight-or-flight) to parasympathetic activity (rest-and-digest). This shift is measurable: heart rate variability increases, cortisol levels fall, and prefrontal function improves. These are not placebo effects. They are physiological interventions with documented mechanisms — the kind of evidence base that surgeons rightly require before adopting any practice.

Building a Personal Stress Protocol

Rather than applying stress management strategies reactively — in the moment of crisis, when cognitive resources are most depleted — the most effective approach is to build a personal stress protocol in advance: a specific sequence of tools, matched to the specific situations in your surgical day, that you execute with the same automaticity as a pre-operative checklist. The pre-case breathing sequence. The post-rounding movement break. The mid-clinic journal entry. The structured boundary around evening messages. These are not aspirational. They are scheduled, specific, and owned.

◆ Dr. Priya | The Pre-Operative Reset

Dr. Priya began practicing a thirty-second breathing sequence before each case: three slow, complete breaths, eyes closed, with a deliberate scan of tension in her neck, shoulders, and hands. She had read about the pre-performance routines of elite athletes and recognized the parallel. Before long it became as automatic as scrubbing. Her circulator noticed that the OR atmosphere was consistently calmer from the moment she arrived at the table. Dr. Priya noticed that her first moves in each case were more deliberate and precise. The thirty seconds was not magic. It was neural priming — and it worked.

◆ Dr. Sandra | The Afternoon Walk

Between clinic and the afternoon's administrative block, Dr. Sandra began taking a ten-minute walk — outside, regardless of weather. She told her MA she was unavailable for those ten minutes. She did not check her phone. She walked without destination. At first it felt like time she could not afford. Within three weeks, her afternoon sessions were measurably more productive — she was clearer, faster, and less irritable — in ways that more than recovered the ten minutes. The walk was not a luxury. It was an investment in the quality of the four hours that followed it.

◄ Reflection & Journaling Prompts

1. *Describe your current surgical day in terms of stress load and recovery opportunities. Where are the natural breaks? Where could brief interventions be inserted without disrupting the schedule?*

2. *What body-based stress response do you most commonly experience during high-demand periods — tension, shallow breathing, gastrointestinal symptoms, something else? Which of the body-based strategies in this chapter directly addresses that response?*

3. *Design your personal stress protocol for a typical surgical day: at least three specific interventions, each matched to a specific moment in your schedule. Make them concrete and achievable.*

4. *What has prevented you from adopting stress management practices previously? Name the specific barrier — not the general one ('no time') but the specific one ('my MA schedules cases back to back with no buffer').*

5. *Who in your surgical environment could you enlist as a co-creator of a more recovery-friendly daily structure? What would you ask of them specifically?*

CHAPTER TEN
– EXPANDED

THE ROLE OF SLEEP, NUTRITION, AND MOVEMENT

The three biological foundations
of sustainable surgical performance

Sleep: The Non-Negotiable Foundation

The surgeon who operates on five hours of sleep is not demonstrating resilience. She is demonstrating the kind of chronic impairment that the medical system she works in would not accept in any other context. We have mandatory rest periods for airline pilots because we understand that fatigue compromises performance in high-stakes environments. The surgical environment is no less high-stakes. And yet the culture of surgical training — with its historical embrace of sleep deprivation as a rite of passage — has normalized a level of fatigue that, by any objective measure, represents an impairment. Sleep restriction studies show measurable cognitive impairment after as few as six nights of six hours of sleep — impairment comparable to 24-48 hours of total sleep deprivation. The surgeon experiencing this impairment cannot accurately assess it. She feels relatively fine. The neurocognitive data tell a different story.

Nutrition as Clinical Infrastructure

The surgeon who skips breakfast, eats lunch at 3 p.m. from a vending machine, and arrives home too depleted to cook is not managing her nutrition — she is managing her body's emergency systems. Glucose is the brain's primary fuel, and blood glucose instability — the predictable consequence of erratic, poor-quality eating — produces predictable cognitive consequences: impaired concentration, emotional dysregulation, and the fatigue that drives the mid-afternoon crash that becomes another source of burnout acceleration. The nutritional intervention does not require a dietitian or an elaborate protocol. It requires treating food as the clinical necessity it is — preparing it with the same priority as clinical preparation, and consuming it at intervals that maintain the metabolic stability necessary for sustained cognitive performance.

Movement as Neurological Medicine

The evidence base for exercise as an intervention for burnout, stress, depression, and anxiety is among the strongest in behavioral medicine. A single thirty-minute session of moderate-intensity aerobic exercise produces measurable increases in brain-derived neurotrophic factor (BDNF) — a protein that promotes neuronal growth and connectivity, the same biological processes that are suppressed by chronic stress. Regular exercise reduces amygdala reactivity, improves prefrontal function, promotes hippocampal neurogenesis, and normalizes the HPA axis dysregulation that underlies burnout. For the surgeon who has been sedentary during her burnout — and most burned-out surgeons have abandoned their exercise routines because they feel like luxuries — the reintroduction of movement is not a quality-of-life enhancement. It is a clinical intervention.

◆ Dr. Amara | Sleep Architecture

When Dr. Amara began tracking her sleep with a consumer device, she was surprised by what the data revealed. She was averaging 5.4 hours per night on weekdays, with a recovery surge to 7.5 hours on weekend nights — a pattern the device flagged as 'social jet lag,' a rhythm-disrupting inconsistency with documented metabolic and cognitive consequences. She made one structural change: a consistent bedtime, seven nights per week, that allowed for seven hours of sleep regardless of the next day's schedule. The first two weeks required discipline. The improvement in her morning cognitive clarity was detectable by week three and remarkable by week six.

◆ Dr. Michelle | The Nutrition Reset

Dr. Michelle spent a Sunday afternoon cooking four days of lunches. Not complicated meals — rice, roasted vegetables, protein, simple sauces. She put them in containers in her clinic refrigerator on Monday morning. For the first time in months, she ate actual food at actual lunch, at an actual table, for twenty actual minutes, three days in a row. The difference in her afternoon energy was so marked that she found herself wondering what she had actually been running on before. She had not changed her schedule. She had changed the quality of the fuel she was giving herself to run on. The change was immediate, measurable, and required nothing from her institution.

Reflection & Journaling Prompts

1. *Complete a 7-day sleep audit: record your actual sleep time each night, your morning energy score (1-10), and any notable cognitive or emotional symptoms. What pattern do you observe?*

2. *Describe your typical daily nutritional intake honestly. What are the gaps? What is the most achievable single change that would have the greatest impact on your cognitive and emotional stability?*

3. *What is your current relationship with movement? If exercise has diminished or disappeared from your life, when did it leave — and what did its departure coincide with?*

4. *Design a movement protocol that fits your actual schedule — not the ideal version of your schedule, but the real one. Start with the minimum effective dose: what is the smallest commitment you would actually keep?*

5. *If sleep, nutrition, and movement are clinical infrastructure for your surgical performance, what would it mean for your institution to take responsibility for supporting them? What specifically would you ask for?*

CHAPTER ELEVEN – EXPANDED

REBUILDING MENTAL WELLNESS

*The slow, deliberate, deeply worthwhile
work of returning to yourself*

Mental wellness, for the surgeon, is not a state that is achieved and then maintained without effort. It is a living system — dynamic, responsive, and requiring ongoing attention in the same way that surgical skill requires ongoing practice. The surgeon who reaches a period of recovery from burnout and then assumes the work is done will find herself back in the cycle, often faster than she returned from it the previous time. The work of mental wellness is not a project with a completion date. It is a practice with a daily commitment.

The Role of Therapy in Surgical Burnout Recovery

Despite the robust evidence for its effectiveness, psychotherapy remains underutilized among burned-out physicians — primarily due to the stigma and confidentiality concerns documented in research. For the surgeon experiencing significant burnout, particularly burnout complicated by secondary depression, moral injury, or trauma, therapy is not a luxury or a sign of failure. It is the appropriate clinical intervention.

The specific therapeutic modalities with the strongest evidence for physician burnout include: Cognitive Behavioral Therapy (CBT), which directly addresses the perfectionist and catastrophizing thought patterns that perpetuate the burnout cycle; Acceptance and Commitment Therapy (ACT), which helps the surgeon reconnect with her core values and build psychological flexibility; and Mindfulness-Based Stress Reduction (MBSR), which addresses the underlying neurological dysregulation of chronic stress. All three are available in formats — including brief, intensive, and telehealth versions — that are compatible with surgical schedules.

For surgeons concerned about confidentiality, the Physician Support Line (1-888-409-0141) offers free, confidential peer support by physicians, for physicians. The American Foundation for Suicide Prevention maintains resources specifically for healthcare providers. Many state medical societies maintain confidential physician health programs. The resources exist. Using them is not weakness — it is the same rational help-seeking behavior that we recommend to our patients every day.

Self-Compassion as a Clinical Skill

Self-compassion — defined by researcher Kristin Neff as treating oneself with the same kindness, care, and understanding that one would offer a good friend in a difficult situation — is among the most evidence-supported interventions for preventing and recovering from burnout. And it is among the most counterintuitive for surgeons, who have been trained to hold themselves to standards they would never apply to a struggling colleague.

Self-compassion is not self-indulgence. It is not lowering the standard. Research consistently shows that self-compassionate individuals hold themselves to high standards — but respond to failures with correction rather than condemnation, with curiosity rather than shame. They are more resilient after setbacks, more willing to take the risks that growth requires, and — critically for this context — significantly more protected against burnout than those who default to harsh self-criticism.

◆ Dr. Priya | The Self-Compassion Letter

At the recommendation of her therapist, Dr. Priya wrote a letter to herself about her post-operative complication case — the one she had been reviewing and re-reviewing for months. The instruction was to write it as though she were addressing a dear friend and respected colleague who had experienced exactly the same complication and was torturing herself with exactly the same questions. She wrote for forty minutes. She described the complexity of the case. She acknowledged the reasonableness of the decisions that had been made. She named what had been learned. She told her friend that she was a good surgeon who had faced a difficult case, and that the response to the complication — the careful management, the transparent communication with the family, the immediate technical review — had been exemplary. She cried while she was writing it. When she finished, she read it as though it had been written for her. Because it had. For the first time in four months, she felt something release.

Building a Sustainable Emotional Practice

The emotional self-care practices that support mental wellness are not a single intervention but a system — multiple practices, distributed across the week, that collectively address the emotional processing, relational connection, expressive release, and restorative recovery that burnout has depleted. The following framework is designed to be implemented incrementally — one practice per week, building to a comprehensive system over a month.

Week One: The Five-Minute Journal

Each evening, write for five minutes — not about events, but about feelings. What emotion was most present today? What triggered it? What does it tell you about what you need? This is not analysis — it is observation. The goal is simply to give emotional experience a channel of expression rather than allowing it to accumulate, unprocessed, in the nervous system.

Week Two: The Connection Commitment

Identify one relationship that has been neglected during your burnout period and make one specific contact this week — not a message, but a genuine, present interaction. Phone call, dinner, a walk. The relationship is both an end in itself and a vehicle for the neurochemical regulation that genuine connection produces.

Week Three: The Expressive Practice

Introduce one expressive activity — creative, physical, or playful — that has no professional purpose whatsoever. The painting that will not be published. The run that has no training goal. The meal cooked for the pleasure of cooking rather than the necessity of eating. The purpose is the experience of existing outside of the surgical role for a defined period of time each week.

Week Four: The Digital Detox Window

Establish a two-hour digital-free period each day — ideally in the evening, before sleep. No email. No social media. No professional messaging. No news. The cognitive and emotional clutter that digital connectivity generates is a documented burnout accelerant. The absence of it — even briefly — allows the nervous system to begin the decompression that sleep requires.

➡ Reflection & Journaling Prompts

1. *What is your current relationship with professional mental health support — therapy, peer support, counseling? What has prevented you from accessing it if you have not? What would it take to change that?*

2. *Write the self-compassion letter described in Dr. Priya's scenario — addressed to a colleague experiencing exactly your current situation. Then read it as written for yourself.*

3. *Which of the four weekly practices in the Sustainable Emotional Practice framework is most absent from your current life? What is the smallest version of that practice you could commit to this week?*

4. *What does your inner critic say to you when you make a mistake? Now rewrite that inner critic's message in the voice of the most compassionate, wise mentor you have ever had.*

5. *How have you defined 'having it together' in your professional life? What parts of yourself have you hidden or suppressed in order to maintain that definition? What would it cost — and what would it free — to let them be visible?*

BOUNDARIES THAT PROTECT YOUR ENERGY

*The skill that will determine whether
your career is sustainable or not*

Why Boundaries Are Not Selfish

The surgeon who maintains firm professional boundaries is not protecting herself at her patients' expense. She is protecting her patients by maintaining the conditions under which she can provide consistently excellent care. The surgeon who answers every message at every hour, who never says no to an additional commitment, who treats her own time and energy as an inexhaustible commons — this surgeon is not more dedicated. She is less sustainable. And the patients who depend on her over the next twenty years of her career are poorly served by the performance she can sustain in the next twenty months without boundaries. The ethical argument for boundaries is not complicated: sustainable care requires a sustainable carer.

The Boundary Conversation

Setting a boundary is a communication act — and like all communication acts, it can be done well or poorly, clearly or ambiguously, kindly or unkindly. The boundary that is communicated clearly and respectfully is far more likely to be honored than the one that is enforced through passive withdrawal or non-response. Many surgeons avoid boundary conversations because they are uncomfortable — and then enforce boundaries through behavior that creates more conflict than the conversation would have. The discomfort of a direct boundary statement lasts seconds. The conflict of an enforced boundary without communication can last months.

Institutional Boundaries: The Larger Fight

Individual boundaries are necessary but not sufficient. The surgeon who sets excellent personal limits while working within an institution that has no structural support for those limits will find herself in a constant defensive battle. Institutional advocacy for sustainable working conditions — adequate staffing, protected time for administrative work, schedule transparency, parental leave that does not result in career penalty — is a collective responsibility that individual surgeons, particularly those in positions of seniority, have an obligation to pursue. The boundaries that the current generation of senior surgeons establishes will shape the conditions in which the next generation practices. This is not abstraction. It is legacy.

♦ Dr. Amara | The Time Cutoff

Dr. Amara's boundary was a simple one: no non-urgent professional communication after 8 p.m. She announced it at a department meeting, quietly and without apology, as a scheduling update. She changed her email signature to include her availability hours. She turned off professional notifications on her personal phone after 8 p.m. In the first week, a resident sent a message at 9:15 p.m. about a non-urgent scheduling question and waited, anxiously, for a response that did not come. Dr. Amara responded at 7:30 the next morning. The resident was fine. The answer was the same as it would have been at 9:15 p.m. And Dr. Amara had slept three hours better than she had the week before.

♦ Dr. Sandra | The Workload Conversation

When her department chair asked her to lead a new quality improvement initiative — the fourth major committee assignment in two years — Dr. Sandra said something she had spent two weeks preparing: 'I am genuinely interested in this work. I am also currently at capacity in ways that would prevent me from doing it well. If you can help me exit or reduce one of my current commitments, I would be glad to take this on. Otherwise, I am not able to do justice to either initiative.' The chair looked at her for a moment. Then he said, 'Which one would you like to step back from?' It was, she said later, the most professionally effective conversation she had in that academic year.

✏ Reflection & Journaling Prompts

1. *Map your current professional boundaries — or the absence of them. Where specifically are you available when you should not be? Where are you saying yes when no would be more honest?*

2. *Draft the boundary conversation you have been avoiding. Write exactly what you would say, to exactly the person who needs to hear it. Practice it until it feels clear and respectful.*

3. *Which of your current commitments is most draining relative to the value it returns — to your career, your patients, your community? What would it take to exit or reduce it?*

4. *What institutional boundary advocacy — for yourself or your colleagues — have you been avoiding because it felt too large or too risky? What is the smallest step toward that advocacy you could take this month?*

5. *Think about the boundaries of the senior surgeons you admire most. What do they protect? How do they communicate those protections? What can you learn from their example?*

CHAPTER THIRTEEN – EXPANDED

RECONNECTING WITH JOY AND MEANING

*Finding your way back to the reason
you chose this life*

The Neuroscience of Meaning

Meaning is not merely a philosophical concept — it is a neurobiological one. Research in positive psychology and neuroscience has identified that experiences of meaning activate the brain's reward circuitry — including the same dopaminergic pathways that are depleted by burnout. This means that reconnecting with meaningful experiences is not simply emotionally beneficial. It is neurologically restorative. It begins to repair the very chemistry that burnout has disrupted. The surgeon who dismisses the pursuit of joy and meaning as 'soft' while experiencing burnout is declining a neurobiological intervention with documented efficacy.

The Case for Small Joys

One of the most counterproductive beliefs in burnout recovery is that joy must be large and dramatic to be restorative — that what is needed is a transformative vacation or a significant life change, and that smaller pleasures are insufficient. The research suggests otherwise. Psychologist Sonja Lyubomirsky's work on the 'hedonic baseline' demonstrates that the frequency of positive emotional experiences is a stronger predictor of wellbeing than their intensity. The surgeon who experiences ten small joys across a week — the morning run, the good coffee, the resident's breakthrough, the dinner cooked with care — builds a more robust wellbeing architecture than one who pursues a single large positive experience and then returns to an unchanged daily life.

Purpose Beyond the Operative Field

For many surgeons, the loss of meaning in burnout feels total — as though the entire edifice of purpose has collapsed. This is rarely accurate upon examination. What has typically occurred is that meaning has narrowed: the surgeon who once found meaning in teaching, in research, in clinical innovation, in her family and community, has collapsed all of those sources into the single domain of operative performance — and when operative performance begins to feel meaningless, everything collapses with it. The recovery of meaning is often a process of re-expansion — returning to the broader sources of purpose that the burnout cycle progressively eliminated.

♦ Dr. Michelle | The Teaching Moment

The turning point for Dr. Michelle did not come in the operating room. It came in a mentoring session with a second-year resident — a young Black woman who had sought her out specifically because there was no one else in the department who looked like her. The conversation lasted ninety minutes. Dr. Michelle shared things she had never shared with a trainee — the difficulties, the doubts, the invisible weight of being first. The resident looked at her with something that Dr. Michelle could only describe as gratitude and recognition. 'Knowing you've done it,' the resident said, 'makes me believe I can.' Dr. Michelle walked back to her office feeling something she had not felt in eighteen months: genuinely necessary. Not merely competent. Necessary.

♦ Dr. Kezia | The Return to Running

Dr. Kezia had run competitively in college. She had given up running gradually — first the races, then the long training runs, then the short ones, until she was not running at all and had not noticed the precise moment it stopped. She returned to it on a Tuesday in March, during her second year of intentional burnout recovery. She ran for twelve minutes before needing to stop. She felt simultaneously ridiculous and deeply glad to be there. Three months later she ran a 10K — her first in nine years. Crossing the finish line produced a feeling she struggled to name: not pride exactly, though pride was there. More like recognition. She had found, in that twelve-minute run, something she had been looking for in the hospital for two years: a version of herself that existed before surgery, and that surgery had not consumed.

⇒ Reflection & Journaling Prompts

1. *What did you love before you loved surgery — or along-side it, before burnout crowded it out? Where is that thing now? What would it take to return to it?*

2. *List ten small joys that are available to you in your current daily life — not the ones that require significant time or money, but the ones that are already there if you are present enough to notice them.*

3. *Name three sources of meaning beyond operative performance that burnout has diminished. What would it take to re-access each one?*

4. *Write the story of why you chose surgery — the real story, the one from before you had language for what you were feeling. Who were you then? What were you reaching for? Is that thing still present? Where?*

5. *Design a 'joy practice' for the next thirty days: one specific intentional joy per day, scheduled in advance. Write them down. Treat them as non-negotiable appointments with yourself.*

CHAPTER FOURTEEN – EXPANDED

DESIGNING A SUSTAINABLE FUTURE

*The architectural work of building
a career that will last a lifetime*

Sustainability as a Design Problem

The most effective sustainable surgical careers are not accidents. They are designed — through deliberate decisions about workload, boundaries, recovery, community, and the daily practices that maintain the person inside the surgeon. The surgeon who does not design her career will have her career designed for her — by institutional demands, cultural expectations, and the relentless gravity of a profession that will absorb every available unit of time and energy if none is protected. Design is not selfishness. It is the condition for a career that lasts, and that serves well, for the decades it is meant to.

The Five-Year Sustainable Practice Vision

A useful design exercise is to project five years forward and describe, in specific detail, what a sustainable practice would look like: How many operative days? What call schedule? What research and teaching commitments? What boundaries? What recovery practices? What does your family life look like? What is your energy level at the end of an average week? This vision is not a fantasy — it is a design target. And the gap between the current reality and the five-year vision is the design problem that the strategies in this book are tools to solve.

Sustainable Excellence in Practice

The surgeons who sustain excellence across long careers are not those who sacrifice most comprehensively. They are those who have learned to be extraordinarily selective about what they sacrifice and what they protect. They decline strategically. They delegate effectively. They build teams that extend their capacity rather than simply adding to their load. They rest deliberately. They invest in relationships that restore rather than drain. They have a clear and stable sense of professional identity that does not collapse under institutional pressure or professional setback. They are, in the fullest sense, sustainable — and their patients, their trainees, and their families benefit from that sustainability across decades.

◆ Dr. Amara | The Five-Year Vision

Dr. Amara spent a Saturday morning writing her five-year vision — not her career goals, which she had documented for promotion purposes, but her sustainability vision: what she wanted her practice and her life to actually look like when both were working. The document was four pages. It described a practice with three operative days per week and two days protected for research, teaching, and administrative work. A call schedule that included guaranteed recovery days. A committee load capped at two. A morning that began with thirty minutes of movement before the hospital. A marriage that felt like a partnership. Children who experienced her as present. She read it back and recognized that none of it was unreasonable. And she recognized that none of it was her current reality. The gap between the two became the map.

◆ Dr. Priya | Building Forward

As she transitioned from fellowship to her first attending position, Dr. Priya negotiated her contract with explicit attention to sustainability: call schedule, operative volume, protected research time, and — after considerable internal debate — a clause about committee expectations in her first two years. She had been told by a mentor that the time to negotiate sustainability is before accepting a position, not after discovering three years in that the position is unsustainable. She arrived to her first week as an attending with a design. Not a perfect one. But a conscious one. That distinction, she would later say, made all the difference.

➡ Reflection & Journaling Prompts

1. *Write your five-year sustainable practice vision in specific, operational detail. Not career goals — sustainability goals. What does a well-designed professional life look like for you?*

2. *What is the gap between your current practice and your sustainability vision? List the three most significant differences. For each one, identify one specific action that would begin to close the gap.*

3. *What are you currently designing — consciously or unconsciously — in your professional life? If someone observed your choices over the past year, what design would they infer?*

4. *What would you negotiate differently if you were accepting your current position today, knowing what you now know about burnout and sustainability?*

5. *Who in your professional network has built a surgical career that you would describe as genuinely sustainable and excellent? What can you learn from the specific choices they have made?*

CHAPTER FIFTEEN
– EXPANDED

THE ROLE OF COMMUNITY
AND SUPPORT SYSTEMS

*The science of connection — and why the surgeon
who goes it alone will not go as far*

Social Connection as Neurobiological Medicine

The human need for connection is not a weakness or a preference. It is a biological imperative with documented physiological mechanisms. Social connection activates the opioid, oxytocin, and dopamine systems that provide the neurochemical counterbalance to the cortisol and adrenaline of chronic stress. Isolation, conversely, activates the brain's threat response — because, for a social species, isolation signals danger. The burned-out surgeon who withdraws from community is depriving herself of the neurobiological resource most effective at counteracting the neurochemical damage of burnout. The isolation is understandable. It is also counterproductive.

Building Community in a Profession That Resists It

The surgical culture — with its hierarchy, its competitive evaluation structures, its historical celebration of individual performance, and its stigmatization of vulnerability — is not designed to produce community. It is designed to produce individual excellence, in conditions that often work against the social connection that sustains it. Building genuine community within this culture requires intentionality: seeking out peers who are willing to be honest rather than performed; finding mentors who will speak truth rather than inspire performance; creating structures — peer groups, support circles, regular check-ins — that make connection a scheduled reality rather than an aspiration.

The Mentor's Role in Burnout Prevention

Research on burnout in surgery consistently identifies effective mentorship as one of the strongest protective factors — across training levels, career stages, and specialty areas. The mentor who creates the conditions for honest conversation, who normalizes the difficulty of the surgical life, who models sustainable practice through her own choices, and who explicitly gives permission to struggle without shame — this mentor changes the trajectory of careers. For those who are now senior enough to serve in this role: the mentorship you provide is not an addition to your legacy. It is a central part of it.

◆ Dr. Sandra | The Senior Colleague

The moment that shifted Dr. Sandra's relationship with community was the day her senior colleague — a surgeon fifteen years her senior — sat down in her office, closed the door, and said: 'I want to tell you something I wish someone had told me fifteen years ago.' He spent the next thirty minutes describing his own burnout — the year he had nearly left surgery, the marriage that had nearly ended, the intervention of a mentor who had done exactly what he was now doing for Dr. Sandra. 'The strongest thing I ever did,' he said, 'was ask for help.' She had not expected this from him — this surgeon who had always appeared invulnerable and entirely in command. His vulnerability did not diminish him in her eyes. It made him the most important mentor she had ever had.

◆ Dr. Michelle | The Community She Built

When Dr. Michelle could not find the community she needed within her institution, she built one. She reached out to eight Black female surgeons across the country — people she had met at conferences, connected with through professional networks, or been introduced to by mutual colleagues. She proposed a monthly video call: no agenda, no presentations, no performance. Just an hour of honest conversation among people who understood the specific landscape each was navigating. Three years later, the group had grown to twenty-two members. It had produced three collaborations, two publications, one departmental policy change, and — by the most conservative count — hundreds of instances of a burned-

out surgeon feeling less alone at exactly the moment she needed it most.

⟜ Reflection & Journaling Prompts

1. *Who are the three people in your professional life who know the full truth of your experience right now — not the performed version, but the real one? If fewer than three names come to mind, what does that tell you?*

2. *Describe the mentor who has most shaped your professional life. What specifically did they do — not in terms of career advice, but in terms of how they showed up for you as a person? How are you doing that for someone else?*

3. *What community do you belong to that exists outside your institutional hierarchy? If the answer is 'none,' what is the smallest step toward building one?*

4. *What would you need to share honestly with a trusted colleague or peer group that you have not yet been able to share? What is the barrier? What would it cost to cross it?*

5. *If you are in a position of seniority, describe one specific thing you could do this month to improve the community conditions for a more junior colleague or trainee experiencing burnout.*

CHAPTER SIXTEEN – EXPANDED

THRIVING, NOT JUST SURVIVING

What flourishing actually looks
like for the surgeon who has done the work

Defining Thriving for the Surgeon

Thriving, in the context of this book, is not the absence of difficulty. Surgery is inherently difficult — and the surgeon who expects otherwise will be perpetually disappointed. Thriving is the presence of sufficient internal and external resources to engage with that difficulty from a position of genuine capacity rather than depletion. It is the ability to experience a hard day and then recover — fully, relatively quickly — rather than adding it to an accumulating deficit. It is the ability to care about a patient without being destroyed by their suffering. To make a mistake and learn from it without being consumed by it. To achieve something meaningful and actually feel the satisfaction, rather than immediately redirecting to the next demand.

The Longitudinal View

The surgeon who is committed to thriving rather than merely surviving is making a choice about the arc of her career — not just its current chapter. Research on physician career satisfaction shows that the habits established in the first decade of practice are strong predictors of career trajectory across the subsequent decades. The surgeon who establishes sustainable practices early — who learns to set limits, to recover, to maintain relationships, to protect the person inside the professional — is building the foundation for a career that remains genuinely excellent across its full length. The surgeon who powers through on sheer discipline and sacrifices everything for the early career is borrowing against a future that becomes increasingly difficult to repay.

What Flourishing Looks Like in Practice

Flourishing in surgery is specific. It looks like arriving to the OR with genuine presence — not just physical presence, but cognitive and emotional availability. It looks like the resident who asks a question and receives not a transaction but a teaching moment, because the attending has the capacity to be genuinely curious about another person's learning. It looks like the patient who feels not just treated but seen — because the surgeon has retained the empathy that burnout had begun to erode. It looks like a career in which each decade builds upon the last, rather than each year costing more than the previous one. And it looks like a person — not just a surgeon — who goes home at the end of the day with something remaining. Something for the people she loves. Something for herself.

Something that replenishes overnight and is ready to begin again in the morning.

◆ Dr. Amara | What Thriving Looks Like

Two years after the Saturday morning she mapped her burnout cycle, Dr. Amara was asked by a junior colleague to describe what had changed. She thought about it carefully before answering. 'I still work hard,' she said. 'I still have difficult days. I still feel the weight of what this work costs. But the difference is — I can feel the weight without being crushed by it. I have enough margin that a hard day does not become a hard week automatically. I come home and there is actually something left when I walk through the door. That,' she said, 'is what changed. Not the surgery. The space around it.'

◆ Dr. Priya | The Letter She Wrote Her Younger Self

In the year she accepted her attending position, Dr. Priya wrote a letter to her first-year resident self — the one who had been brilliant and eager and entirely unprepared for what the training would cost. She told her: that the difficulty she was about to experience was real, and not a sign of inadequacy. That the moments she would want to quit would not mean she had chosen wrongly. That the mentors who seemed invulnerable were not. That rest was not laziness. That asking for help was not failure. That the surgeon she would become was worth protecting — not as a means to surgical excellence, but as a person, in her own right, with her own irreducible worth. She sealed the letter and put it in her desk. She plans to give it to the first resident who reminds her of herself.

➡ Reflection & Journaling Prompts

1. *Describe what thriving would look like for you in specific, operational terms — not as an abstraction, but as a daily reality. What would be different from your current experience?*

2. *What is the single most important change you could make — right now, this week — that would most directly move you from your current position toward thriving?*

3. *Write a letter to a junior colleague who is about to begin the kind of period you have just navigated. What do you wish someone had told you? What would it mean to give that gift?*

4. *Looking back over this book, which chapter or concept has been most significant for you? What specifically has it shifted in how you understand your situation?*

5. *What is your commitment to yourself, beginning today? Write it in specific, behavioral terms — not aspirations, but actions. Sign it. Keep it where you will see it.*

CONCLUSION – EXPANDED

A LETTER TO THE SURGEON WHO HAS READ THIS FAR

And a charge to carry it forward

You have reached the end of this book. And if you have done the reflection work — the journaling, the honest assessment, the difficult conversations with yourself — you have done something more than read. You have begun. The beginning, in burnout recovery, is no small thing. Many surgeons know the information about burnout for years before they act on it. The gap between knowing and doing is where careers quietly erode and where the cycle repeats. You have chosen to close that gap.

Let us summarize what has been true throughout these pages: Burnout is not a character flaw. It is not evidence of insufficient commitment or inadequate resilience. It is the predictable, documented, mechanistically understood consequence of sustained demand without adequate recovery

— in a professional culture that has historically rewarded the behaviors most likely to produce it. Understanding this does not remove your agency. It properly distributes the responsibility — between you and the structure you inhabit — and allows you to address both with the tools that are actually effective.

The Work Ahead

The recovery from burnout is not a linear ascent. There will be weeks that feel like genuine progress and weeks that feel like relapse. There will be structural changes you make that hold, and ones that are eroded by institutional pressure, unexpected demands, or your own trained instincts toward overcommitment. This is not failure. This is the normal pattern of any significant behavioral and structural change. What matters is not that the progress is smooth — it will not be — but that the direction is consistent.

The five surgeons whose stories have accompanied you through this book — Dr. Amara, Dr. Priya, Dr. Michelle, Dr. Sandra, Dr. Kezia — are not finished stories. They are ongoing ones. They still have hard days. They still face structural conditions that are not what they should be. They still, occasionally, find themselves at the beginning of the cycle and recognize it faster than they once did. What has changed is the speed and quality of the recognition, the size of the toolkit, the presence of the community, and the clarity of the permission: to rest, to set limits, to be a person first and a surgeon in service of that person.

Your Responsibility to Those Who Come After

You have been shaped by every surgeon who came before you — by their choices about culture, mentorship, and the standards they set for what the surgical life should cost. You are now, in turn, shaping the surgeons who come after you. The resident on your service is watching how you manage your energy, your boundaries, your humanity. The medical student rotating through your operating room is forming her first impressions of what a surgical career looks like from the inside. The junior colleague who is quietly struggling is waiting to see whether you are someone she can approach with honesty.

The culture of surgical burnout will not change through individual recovery alone. It will change when surgeons who have done their own work become the mentors who give permission, the chiefs who protect time, the senior colleagues who close the door and say: 'I want to tell you something I wish someone had told me.' The individual work and the cultural work are not separate. They are the same work, across different scales.

♦ Dr. Michelle | The Legacy

Four years after beginning her own burnout recovery, Dr. Michelle was asked to give grand rounds on physician wellness at a regional academic center. She agreed — and then spent two weeks writing the talk she wished she had heard ten years earlier. She named structural barriers by name. She described the gender-specific burden with data and with personal experience. She named the racial dimension without softening it. And she told her own story — the year she had nearly left surgery, the peer group that had saved her, the one therapy session in which she had finally cried in front of another person about what the work was costing. After the talk, six people approached her privately. Two of them were senior surgeons who said they had never heard those words spoken out loud in a professional setting. Four were residents who said they had needed to hear it. One was a program director who said she planned to change her program's wellness curriculum. Dr. Michelle drove home from that talk and felt, for the first time in her career, that her story had not been only hers to carry.

> *"The surgeon who heals herself becomes the surgeon who changes the culture. That is not a small thing. That is, in the fullest sense, legacy."*

Go rest. Go recover. Go back to the OR when you are ready — not the version of ready that means 'tolerable,' but the version that means 'genuinely present.' Your patients deserve that version. Your trainees deserve it. Your family deserves it. And so do you — not as a reward for good behavior, but as a right that belongs to you simply because you are a human being who has chosen an extraordinarily demanding and extraordinarily important way of spending a life.

You became a surgeon because something in you knew this was the work. That something is still there. This book has been an attempt to help you find your way back to it — and to build, around it, a life that can sustain it for as long as you want to practice.

The work continues. So do you.

167

— With deep respect, for every surgeon who dares to ask for more than endurance —

The Burnout Cure: Mental Wellness for Busy Lives — The Surgeon's Edition

Robert Amajoyi, MD; Ebere Jill Azumah, MD MPH

ABOUT THE AUTHORS

Dr. Rob

———

President

*Unstuck
Lifestyle
Coaching*

Robert Amajoyi, MD, FACS, FICS, FASCRS

Division Chief, Colon & Rectal Surgery · Grady Memorial Hospital & Morehouse School of Medicine Vice President, International College of Surgeons · Board Member, World Surgical Foundation

Dr. Robert Amajoyi built his life at the edge of two worlds — the operating room and the coaching stage — and refused to choose between them. Inaugural President and co-founder of the Society of Black Colon and Rectal Surgeons. Humanitarian. Philanthropist. A Tony Robbins Protégé. Through Unstuck Lifestyle Coaching, he has guided surgeons and physicians to master career, self, business, and wealth. He wrote this book because he has lived every page of it.

To work with him visit www.unstucklifestyle.com

Ebere Jill Azumah, MD, MPH

FACOG · FICS · Certified Life Coach Harvard T.H. Chan School of Public Health

Dr. Ebere Jill Azumah is a board-certified obstetrician and gynecologist, public health physician, and certified life coach with a Master of Public Health from Harvard. Founder of Azumah Solutions and co-founder of Love Your Menses, Inc. — a global menstrual equity organization — she brings the dual lens of clinical medicine and human transformation to every page of this book.

To work with her visit www.azumahsolutions.com

www.unstucklifestyle.com